Fashions After the Era of Jane Austen

Ackermann's Repository

OF

ARTS, LITERATURE, COMMERCE,

Manufactures, Fashions, and Politics

1821 - 1828

Designed and Edited by

Jody Gayle

Publications of the Past

Publications of the Past, Inc.
PO Box 233
Columbia, MO 65205

For further information email
jody@jodygayle.com
or visit
www.JodyGayle.com

ISBN-13: 978-09884001-3-9
E-Book Edition: ISBN: 978-0-9884001-4-6
Cover: Promenade Dress from *Ackermann's Repository of Arts*, August 1826
Glossary: Dover book, *Ackermann's Costume Plates*

Acknowledgements

My sincerest gratitude to the Philadelphia Museum of Art Library for permission to reintroduce the two-hundred-year-old *Ackermann's Repository of Arts* to a whole new group of readers.

A special thank you to the authors of Regency era fiction, who continue to make the society, customs and fashions of early 19th Century England vivid and vital to several generations of readers.

This book was inspired by the work of Candice Hern. She offers fashion plates for her fans, and this fueled my passion for this project. She has one of the best websites for Regency era information. Answers to almost any question about the Regency era can be found at Candice's website, which will also direct you to other resources. Please visit her web site: www.candicehern.com

Contents

1823

January	53
Morning Dress	
Ball Dress	
February	55
Evening Dress	
Head Dresses	
March	57
Walking Dress	
Evening Dress	
April	59
Morning Dress	
Evening Dress	
May	61
Walking Dress	
Evening Dress	
June	63
Carriage Dress	
Ball Dress	
July	65
Morning Dress	
Ball Dress	
August	67
Evening Dress	
Ball Dress	
September	69
Morning Dress	
Evening Dress	
October	71
Morning Dress	
Ball Dress	
November	73
Head Dresses	
Full Dress	
December	75
Full Dress	
Evening Dress	

1824

January	77
Morning Dress	
Promenade Dress	
February	79
Walking Dress	
Evening Dress	
March	81
Morning Dress	
Evening Dress	
April	83
Dinner Dress	
Ball Dress	
May	85
Morning Dress	
Dinner Dress	
June	87
Promenade Dress	
Ball Dress	
July	89
Promenade Dress	
Opera Dress	
August	91
Morning Dress	
Ball Dress	
September	93
Morning Dress	
Evening Dress	
October	95
Promenade Dress	
Dinner Dress	
November	97
Morning Dress	
Evening Dress	
December	99
Morning Dress	
Evening Dress	

1827

1828

Glossary

"It would be mortifying to the feelings of many ladies, could they be made to understand how little the heart of a man is affected by what is costly or new in their attire... "

— Jane Austen, *Northanger Abbey*

In the time of Jane Austen, the functions of fashionable dress were to draw attention to the wearer, to define his/her social position, to show who he/she is and what he/she is doing. The secondary functions of fashionable dress were modesty, protection against the weather, and appeal to the opposite sex. Fashion can be defined as a general style of dress appropriate for a particular person to wear at a certain time of day, on a special occasion, or for a specific purpose. Fashion is a complex facet of society.

To study the fashions in England during the nineteenth century, one must dedicate time to the highly popular publication the *Repository of Arts, Literature, Commerce, Manufactures, Fashions and Politics*. The *Ackermann's Repository of the Arts* was a monthly British periodical published from 1809-1828 by Rudolph Ackermann. It was a very popular nineteenth century publication devoted to the study of the arts, literature, commerce, manufacturing, politics and fashion and each issue consists of 60-80 pages an issue. It included a significant amount of information provided by the readers, such as personal, poems, opinion pieces and general interest articles.

The fashion plates in the *Repository* could be compared to the contemporary magazine *Vanity Fair*...the *Vanity Fair* of the late Georgian era. The Repository of Arts created an archive of superb hand-colored plates depicting examples of the latest women's fashion. The publication was a guide to dressmakers and their fashionable clients. The fashion descriptions for the plates included details of the type of clothing shown, its style, cut, trim, fabrics used, color, style and accessories.

The fashion plates from the *Repository of the Arts* are well documented on the internet, but few illustrations include the original accompanying text published with the fashion plate. It seems sad that the words of the past are being forgotten. I'm sure there are others, like me, who want to read the fashion descriptions. The illustrations need to be described in the language of their time, because the words add a whole new depth to the illustrations, and most importantly, a glimpse into the culture.

Two hundred years after the era of Jane Austen we are still delighted and inspired by the fashions of nineteenth century England. The illustrations in the *Repository of Arts* magazine were mainly for the haute ton or the very wealthy; however, they still drove what was considered fashionable dress at other levels of society. Jane Austen may or may not have sewn or dressed in these fashions, but she certainly was aware of the *Repository of Arts* magazine during her time.

The intent of this pictorial is to offer images exclusively from the *Ackermann's Repository of Arts*. This provides readers the opportunity to study the fashion plates and read the original accompanying descriptions. It is important to note the descriptions are as they were in the magazine. The punctuation, spelling, sentence structure and even word usage in some instances are vastly different than what we use today; even changing from issue to issue. Considerable effort has been directed at being precise and providing the text as it was originally written. There are many words that were spelled differently throughout the years. Examples include: head-dress, headdress, demi-train, demi-traine, needle-work and needlework. No changes were made to keep the book consistent. The fashion etchings have also not been altered.

It is left to the reader to make their own analyses of the trends and draw their own conclusions from the material provided regarding fashions presented in the *Repository of Arts, Literature, Commerce, Manufactures, Fashions and Politics.*

I do have to note that some of these illustrations are very old, so images aren't necessarily as clear as we may want. Even when the reproductions are imperfect, I think they still add to the idea of traveling back in time.

Ackermann's Repository of Arts

The following article was first published in the first issue of the *Repository of Arts:* January 1809.

This plate is a representation of Mr. Ackermann's Shop, No. 101, Strand, and is the commencement of a series of plates intended to exhibit the principal shops of this great metropolis, in the same manner as the *Microcosm of London* represents the interior of the *public* buildings. It will afford the opportunity of entering into a partial detail of the different manufactures that are exposed in them for sale; and we flatter ourselves will form an useful, as well as interesting, part of our work. This shop stands upon part of the court-yard in front of which was Beaufort-House, formerly a town residence of the noble family whose name it bore, and was one of the great number of mansions which, at no very distant period, lined the bank of the Thames from Templebar to the city of Westminster. The noble and lofty apartments of the house, which commences at the back part of the shop, and a fine oak staircase of considerable dimensions, hear a testimony of its former magnificence. After it had ceased to be the residence of the Beaufort family, it was converted into the Fountain Tavern, a house of great celebrity in former days, and was remarkable from the circumstance of Lord Lovat stopping there to take in refreshment on his way from Westminster-Hall to the Tower, and writing with his diamond ring the following couplet upon a pane of glass in the great room:

> Oh! through what various scenes of life we run,
> Are wicked to great and being great undone!
> Simon Fraser

This room, which is 65 feet in length, 30 in width, and 24 in height, was formerly occupied by Mr. Shipley, brother to the bishop of that name; he kept a most respectable drawing academy here: among his pupils were, Mr. W Parr, who died at Rome, C. Smart, Esq. and the celebrated R. Cosway, Esq. R.A.: the latter had in his possession the pane of glass before-mentioned. A curious, but well-authenticated anecdote is related of Henry Parr's wife (H. Parr succeeded Shipley in this academy) who had been confined to the house upwards of nine years by a paralytic affection, which during that period entirely deprived her of speech. One day, in the absence of her husband, the servant-maid abruptly entering her apartment, told her that the adjoining house was on fire, which had such an effect upon her system, that her powers of utterance returned instantaneously, and she continued to enjoy them again to the day of her death, which did not happen for some year afterwards.

This room is famous on another account, having been the scene of Mr. Thelwall's early political lectures. When the interposition of government put a stop to this exhibition, Mr. A. purchased the lease, and it became once more the peaceful academy of drawing, upon a very extended scale, employing three masters in the separate branches of this art, one for figures, a second for landscape, and a third for architecture. But the increase of Mr. Ackermann's business as a publisher, printseller, and manufacturer of fancy articles, rendered the convenience of this room a warehouse a more desirable object than the profit to be derived from it as an academy. For eight or ten years previous to entering so largely in the fancy business, Mr. A. had been employed in furnishing the principal coachmakers with designs and models for new and improved carriages. Among many instances of his taste and abilities in this line, the state coach built for the Lord Lieutenant of Ireland, in 1790, which cost near 7000/. and one for the Lord Mayor of Dublin in the following year, were designed and modelled by him. It has been said, that Philip Godsal, Esq. who has the model of the Lord Lieutenant's coach, has actually refused one hundred guineas for it, and it is more than probable, he would not sell it for twice that sum.

During the period when the French emigrants were so numerous in this country, Mr. A. was among the first to strike out a liberal and easy mode of employing them, and he had seldom less than fifty noble, priests, and ladies of distinction, at work upon screens, card-racks, flower-stands, and other ornamental fancy-works of a similar nature. Since the decree permitting the return of the emigrants to France, this manufacture has been continued by native artists, who execute the work in a very superior style: but it is impossible in this place to notice the great variety of articles which it embraces. The public are referred to a catalogue of near 100 pages, which conveys every information that can be necessary, and will be our apology for omitting any further observations; we shall therefore only add, that since Mr. A. has given up the academy, he has substituted a portfolio of prints and drawings for the use of pupils and dilitanti, upon the plan of a circulating library of books, the terms of which areas follow: Yearly subscription.

4 Guineas,
Half-yearly ditto.. 2 ditto.
Quarterly ditto... I ditto.

The money paid at the time of subscribing. The subscribers are allowed to take the value of their subscription money in prints or drawings, and may change them as often as they please.

Promenade Dress
January 1821

PROMENADE DRESS

A high gown composed of poplin, of a colour between a ruby and geranium: the bottom of the skirt is trimmed with a very broad fullness of *gros de Naples*, to correspond in colour with the dress; this is finished at each edge with a chain trimming composed of plaited *gros de Naples*. The body is tight to the shape: the long sleeve is rather straight; it falls a good deal over the hand, and is finished at the bottom to correspond with the skirt, but the trimming is not more than a third of the width. The epaulette consists of three full puffs formed by a chain trimming which goes round them. Plain high collar, finished at the edge by a chain. The pelisse corresponds in colour with the gown; it is lined with white sarsnet: the body is made tight to the shape; the waist about the same length as last month, and the sleeve tight. The trimming of the pelisse is a beautiful new material, which has been but just invented: it is exceedingly light and rich; and is simply disposed in a rouleau, which goes all round. The pelisse wraps very much to one side. High collar, which forms at once a collar and a small pelerine. Head-dress, a bonnet made of the silk called *du cape*; it corresponds in colour with the pelisse; the crown is made moderately high; it is finished with ornaments somewhat resembling leaves, which go half way across it; they are edged with *pluche de soie*: the brim is very wide across the forehead, and is a little pointed in front; it slopes gradually down at the sides, and nearly meets under the chin; it is lined with white satin: a row of *pluche de soie* is attached to the edge of the brim, and another is laid on at a little distance from the first; a row also encircles the bottom of the crown, and a bunch of damask roses is placed in front: strings to correspond tie it under the chin. Ermine muff; black leather half-boots, and Limeric gloves.

Evening Dress
January 1821

EVENING DRESS

A round dress, composed of white transparent gauze, over a white satin slip. The bottom of the dress is finished by four rouleaus of pink *du cape*; this is surmounted by a fulness of gauze, disposed in puffs of a novel and pretty form, each ornamented with a bow at top; they are headed by two rouleaus of pink *du cape*. The *corsage* is long in the waist, plain in front, but a little full behind: it is cut moderately low round the bust. The sleeve is perfectly novel in form, and we must refer for it to our print: it is composed of a mixture of gauze and pink *du cape*. A white satin girdle, rather broader before than behind, and clasped in front with a pearl buckle, finishes the dress. The hair is dressed lightly on the forehead, and moderately high behind. Headdress, a pearl tiara, placed rather low on the forehead, and a pearl ornament set very far back on the crown of the head. Necklace and ear-rings, pearl. White satin shoes, and white kid gloves.

We are indebted to Miss Pierpoint, of No. 9, Henrietta-street, Covent-Garden, inventress of the corset à *la Grecque*, for both these dresses.

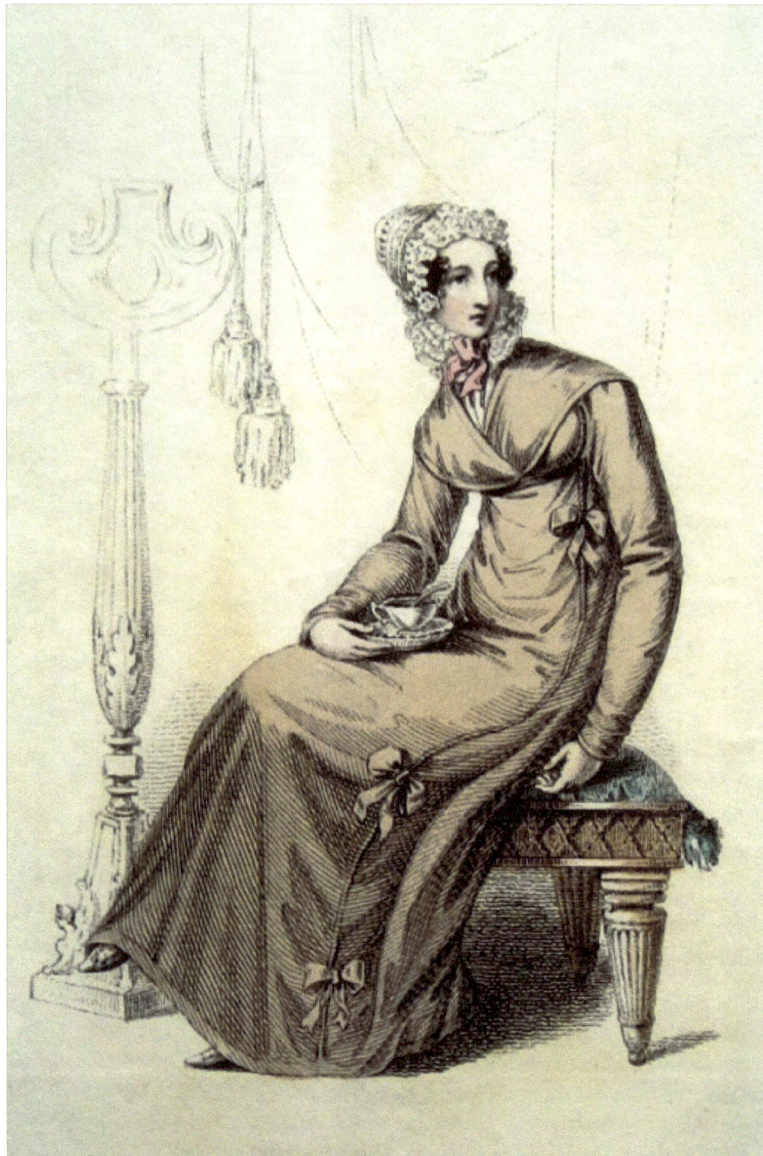

Morning Dress
February 1821

MORNING DRESS

A wrapping dress composed of cachemire: the waist is the usual length; the body comes up to the throat in the back of the neck, but is a little sloped in front, and turns over all round so as to form a pelerine; it wraps across before, and displays a little of the *fichu* worn underneath. The back has a little fullness; it is of a moderate breadth, and a good deal sloped at the sides. The sleeve is easy, but not wide; it is finished at the wrist by folds of *gros de Naples*, to correspond in colour with the dress. The girdle is also of *gros de Naples*; it is rather broad, and fastens with a gold clasp at the side. The skirt is moderately wide; it wraps across to the left side, and is fastened up the front with bows to correspond. Head-dress, a *cornette* composed of full bands of net inserted between plain ones of letting-in lace; the crown is remarkably low; the ears are cut very narrow, and far back; and it fastens with a full bow of pale pink ribbon under the chin. Black kid shoes.

Evening Dress
February 1821

EVENING DRESS

A round dress, composed of Urling's net, over a white satin slip: the dress is finished at the bottom of the skirt with a full *ruche* of net edged with blue zephyreene; a broad *bouillonné* of net surmounts the *ruche*: there is something very novel in the arrangement of this *bouillonné* but we must refer to our print for its form; it is interspersed with blue and white zephyreene ornaments called *crabs*, a name which is very appropriate to their form. The *corsage* is cut moderately low round the bust, and rather long in the waist; it is composed of blue and white zephyreene intermixed; it is ornamented in front on each side of the bust with lace, which is so disposed as to form a fan stomacher; the back is plain; a single fall of lace, set on moderately full, goes round the bust. Short full sleeve, made of net over white satin; the net is disposed in folds, which are edged with blue zephyreene; the last fold is also finished with lace at the edges: they are looped up with bows of blue zephyreene. The front hair is a good deal parted on the forehead; it is dressed in very light curls, and falls low at each side of the face. The hind hair is disposed in braids, which do not come higher than the crown of the head. A pearl bandeau, brought rather forward on the forehead, encircles the head, and a full plume of white ostrich feathers droops to one side: the middle of each feather is covered with a thick down, which gives them a peculiar beauty and richness. Necklace and earrings, pearl. White satin shoes, and white kid gloves. We are indebted to Miss Pierpoint, inventress of the *corset à la Grecque*, of No. 9, Henrietta-street, Covent-Garden, for both these dresses.

Head-Dresses
March 1821

HEAD-DRESSES

No. 1. A Bonnet composed of black *du cape*: it has a low crown, and a very large brim, which is lined with pink zephyreene; the edge of the brim is ornamented with a wreath of black satin, disposed in scalloped folds. A full plume of black marabouts is placed at the right side of the crown, and a bow of the same material as the bonnet is attached to the base of the plume. Black *gros de Naples* strings

No. 2. A *ponceau* velvet bonnet lined with white satin: the brim is deep, but sits close to the face; it is edged with a rouleau of *ponceau* satin; the velvet is laid in full folds on the crown, which is of an oval shape; a small piece of velvet falls into the neck; a bow of the same material is placed in the centre of the crown, and a wreath of full-blown roses goes round the bottom of it. *Ponceau* strings.

No. 3. A white satin hat: the crown is low; the brim is of a very novel shape; it is small, turns up, and is square on the left side, and rounded and much deeper on the right side, where a knot of white satin is placed just under the edge. A plume of white flat ostrich feathers, at the base of which is a full bow of white satin, is attached to the right side of the crown.

No. 4. A hat composed of white figured satin; the crown is low; the brim turns up in front; it is shallow at the sides, but deep over the forehead. A plume of white flat ostrich feathers is placed on the right side, and droops as low as the left shoulder. This hat is worn over a *cornette* of tulle.

No. 5. A small round cap composed of British net, with a very full border of rich lace; a knot of green ribbon is placed at the right ear, and a similar knot over the forehead, with a bouquet of primroses surrounded with foliage.

Evening Dress
March 1821

EVENING DRESS

A round dress composed of pale pink *soie de Londres*, trimmed with pink zephyreene fluted in a scroll pattern. The *corsage* is cut square at the bust, and so as to display the neck a good deal; the back is plain, and laced behind; the front is ornamented with a stomacher, broad at the top, but sloping in a good deal towards the bottom, and coming very little below the waist: it is decorated with pearls. The sleeve is a fulness of net over pink *soie de Londres*; the fulness is confined in the middle by a pink satin ornament. The hair is dressed in loose ringlets on the forehead, and falling low at the sides; the hind hair is cut partly behind, so as to curl in the neck; the remaining part is braided, and brought round the head. Head-dress, a tiara of diamonds and a full plume of marabouts. Necklace and ear-rings, diamonds. White kid gloves, and white satin shoes.

We are indebted to Miss Pierpoint, inventress of the *corset à la Grecque*, of No. 9, Henrietta-street, Covent-Garden, for this elegant dress and the head-dresses which we present this month to our fair subscribers.

Promenade Dress
April 1821

PROMENADE DRESS

A high dress composed of cambric muslin; the bottom of the skirt is trimmed with a very deep flounce of work, above which is a fulness of thin jaconot muslin let in in a broad wave, at each edge of which is a row of embroidery. High body, tight to the shape, made without a collar, but finished at the throat with a full trimming of work. Plain long sleeve, terminated with a triple fall of work. The pelisse worn over this dress is composed of lavender-coloured zephyreene, and lined with white sarsnet; the bottom of the skirt is trimmed with two folds of satin to correspond, and each fold is adorned with a silk cord at the edge. The pelisse wraps a little to the right side, and is fastened down with full bows of zephyreene, corded at the edges with satin. Plain tight body; the waist rather long, and finished in the middle of the back with a full bow and ends of zephyreene. High collar, very much sloped in front. The long sleeve is finished at the bottom with a fulness of satin, above which are satin folds. The half-sleeve is uncommonly novel and pretty: we refer for its form to our print. Head-dress, a bonnet of the same material as the pelisse, mixed with satin: it is of a moderate size; the zephyreene is laid full on the crown, the top of which is adorned with shells; the brim is fluted, and finished at the edge with satin bands, intermixed with small bows: it is lined with pale pink zephyreene. A full plume of round ostrich feathers, lavender and white, is placed to one side, and a broad ribbon to correspond ties it under the chin. British lace veil in imitation of Brussels. Half-boots of lavender-coloured kid, and Limerick gloves.

Full Dress
April 1821

FULL DRESS

A round dress composed of Urling's lace over a white satin slip; the bottom of the skirt is trimmed with a full flounce of lace, headed by a broad rouleau of white satin, and surmounted by demi lozenges of lace, edged with rouleaus of satin. Plain tight body, cut square round the bust; a full plaiting of net goes round; there are three rows behind, but only one in front: it is quilled, so that a part stands up and shades the bosom. A broad white satin sash is tied behind in short bows and long ends. The sleeve is composed of white lace over white satin; the former is disposed in demi lozenges: there are two rows arranged in such a manner as to form a singularly pretty sleeve. The hind hair is plaited, and brought round the crown of the head; the front hair disposed in ringlets, rather low at the sides, and much parted, so as to display the forehead. Head-dress, a pearl crescent, placed over the forehead, but put very far back, and a very full plume of ostrich feathers on the left side. Necklace and earrings, pearls. White satin shoes, and white kid gloves.

We are indebted to Miss Pierpoint, of No. 9, Henrietta-street, Covent-Garden, inventress of the *corset à la Grecque*, for both these dresses.

Fancy Ball Dress
May 1821

FANCY BALL DRESS

A round dress, composed of pink gauze over satin to correspond; at the bottom of the skirt is a wreath of full-blown roses, placed at the edge; above this wreath is a row of shells, embroidered in silver at irregular distances; they are surmounted by bouquets of roses, which are also placed irregularly, with considerable spaces left between. The *corsage* is rather long in the waist; it is cut square round the bust, but is not so low as usual; it fastens behind: a blond tucker *à l' enfant* goes round the bust, and is headed by a very full wreath of blond shells edged with pink satin. Full sleeve of pink gauze over satin; it is disposed in a row of full pulls, which are surrounded by gauze bands edged with satin to correspond; these bands are fastened by small bouquets composed of roses and honeysuckle: a narrow gauze *ruche*, set on very full, terminates the sleeve. The hair is disposed in full soft curls at the sides of the face, and is much parted on the forehead; it is dressed very low behind. Head-dress, a pearl tiara, placed rather far back, and a full plume of white ostrich feathers; they are put at the left side, almost at the back of the head, and droop over the forehead. Ear-rings and necklace, pearls; the latter is a *négligé*, with a knot of pearls depending from it. White kid gloves. White *gros de Naples* slippers, with satin quillings and rosettes.

Head-Dresses
May 1821

HEAD-DRESSES

No, 1. A bonnet composed of white *gros de Naples*; the crown, of a moderate height, is round, and ornamented *en marmotte* with a *gros de Naples* handkerchief, trimmed with Urling's lace, the ends of which fasten under the chin. The brim is large, and trimmed at the edge with a very full quilling of lace. A fancy flower is placed on one side of the crown.

No. 2. A white lace *cornette*: the caul is round and small, but appears high, from being ornamented with what the *marchandes de modes* call a lace gipsy; this goes all round the crown, but stands out from it, and is finished with satin piping. The head-piece is small, and the ears narrow, and cut very far back; double border of broad net, quilled very full. A bouquet of flowers is placed across the caul, and a bow of lilac ribbon fastens the ears under the chin.

No. 3. A blond net *cornette*: the caul is higher than we have recently seen them; it is disposed in folds; the head-piece is small, and the ears rather broad; the border is of blond lace disposed in full flutings. A bunch of lilac ornaments the crown, and white strings fasten it under the chin.

No. 4. A white zephyreene bonnet: the crown is small, and rather of a melon shape, and the brim is very deep; it is finished at the edge with broad blond put on very full, and surmounted by a wreaths of embossed white satin leaves. The crown is surrounded with small bouquets of apple-blossoms, which are placed at regular distances, and just in front is a full bow of zephyreene.

No. 5. A turban composed of blond mixed with white satin: the crown is of blond, and very full, but the fulness is confined by satin folds; the lower part is composed of small tight folds of mingled satin and blond. A blond drapery, tastefully decorated with satin pipings, and edged with blond lace, falls from behind.

We are indebted to Miss Pierpoint, inventress of the *corset à la Grecque*, of No. 9, Henrietta-street, Covent-Garden, for both the fancy ball-dress and the headdresses.

Morning Dress
June 1821

MORNING DRESS

A cambric muslin round dress: the skirt is of an easy fulness, and a good deal gored; it is trimmed at the bottom with flounces of the same material, corded at the edges, and disposed in a bias direction; this trimming is very deep: the body fastens behind, and is tight to the shape; the waist is a little shorter than last month. A falling collar, which partially exposes the throat, is pointed, and slightly embroidered at the edge: long sleeve, moderately wide, and falling very far over the hand; it is terminated by a very novel and pretty cuff, formed of two falls of trimming slightly embroidered at the edge. The epaulette, for which we must refer to our print, is of a very novel form; it is formed entirely of work. Morning *cornette* composed of Urling's lace. Black kid shoes.

Full Dress
June 1821

FULL DRESS

A white satin round dress, finished at the bottom of the skirt with a trimming of oak-leaves formed of the same material, and headed by a wreath of intermingled pale pink and deep rose-coloured china-asters; above which are small bouquets of wild blossoms, placed at regular distances. *Corsage*, plain back, terminated by a short full jacket *à la corset*, laced in front, and a little pointed at the bottom of the waist: the bust, which is cut square, and of a very decorous height, is trimmed with a full quilling of spotted *tulle*, set on double and very deep behind, but single and much narrower in front: short full sleeve, with an epaulette composed of lozenge puffs inserted in plain bands, and finished at the bottom by a cording of white satin. The hair is dressed very low behind, and in thick curls on the temples; it is ornamented with a wreath of wild blossoms, to correspond with those in the trimming of the dress. Necklace and earrings, pearls. White kid gloves, and white corded silk slippers. — We are indebted to

Miss Pierpoint of No. 12, Edwards-street, Portman-square, inventress of the *corset à la Grecque*, for both dresses.

16

Promenade Dress
July 1821

PROMENADE DRESS

A cambric muslin gown, trimmed at the bottom of the skirt with clear muslin bouillonné, let in in waves; each wave is embroidered round the edge, and the trimming is terminated by a full flounce of that sort of work which resembles point lace. High body, tight to the shape, finished round the bust by a narrow wave, to correspond with the trimming of the bottom. Long sleeve, rather tight, terminated by a double fall of work. Small epaulette, composed also of work. The pelisse worn over this dress is made of evening primrose *gros de Naples*, and lined with white sarsnet: the trimming is of the same material as the pelisse. We must refer to our print for the form of the trimming: it is perfectly novel, and has a very striking and tasteful effect. The epaulette is a mixture of satin and *gros de Naples*, disposed to correspond with the trimming. Long sleeve, rather tight, and finished at the hand in a very novel style. High collar, standing out from the throat, so as to display a rich lace ruff. Headdress, a bonnet of white *gros de Naples* lined with white satin, and ornamented with two narrow rouleaus, placed under the edge of the brim; the crown is a moderate height; the brim very deep, and finished at the edge with the new trimming called Lapland moss: a piece of this latter material, which is edged with blond, is very tastefully disposed on the top of the crown, in the middle of which it is clasped by full folds of white satin. A plume of white ostrich feathers, tinged with pink at the edges, is placed on one side, and a white gauze ribbon, spotted with pink, ties it under the chin. Limerick gloves, and kid boots to correspond with the pelisse.

Evening Dress
July 1821

EVENING DRESS

A round dress composed of British net over a white satin slip; the bottom of the skirt is finished with a full double *ruche* of the same material, and this is surmounted by a trimming composed of net puffs; their form is that of a crescent: they are let in irregularly, and to a considerable height. *Corsage* of the usual length, cut square, and moderately high round the bust, which is ornamented by a deep fall of lace, surmounted by a trimming of shells formed of net intermixed with white satin. Short full sleeve to correspond with the trimming of the bottom, and terminated by a fall of lace; the zone is composed of steel net, clasped in front by a steel buckle, cut to resemble diamonds. The hair is parted so as to display nearly the whole of the forehead; it is arranged in light curls, which hang low at the sides of the face. The hind hair is fastened in a simple knot, which does not rise higher than the crown of the head. Head-dress, a pearl tiara placed across the head, and overshadowed by a full plume of white down feathers. Necklace and ear-rings, pearls. White satin shoes, and white kid gloves.

We are indebted to Miss Pier-point of No. 12, Edwards-street, Portman-square, inventress of the corset *a la Grecque*, for both these dresses.

Walking Dress
August 1821

WALKING DRESS

A cambric muslin round dress; the bottom of the skirt is trimmed with a flounce of scolloped work, disposed in deep plaits at some distance from each other, and the spaces between left plain; in the middle of each space is a muslin tab: this trimming is surmounted by another composed of full puffings of muslin, with lozenges between, and a rouleau of muslin at the top. High body, tight to the shape, profusely ornamented with work, and trimmed at the wrists and round the throat with scolloped lace. Spencer of cerulean blue *soic de Londres*: it is tight to the shape; the waist is the usual length, and it is finished with a full bow and ends of the same material, corded with satin in the middle of the back. The bust is formed, in a most becoming manner, by a fold of satin edged with a loop trimming of *soic de Londres*, which goes in a sloping direction from the shoulder to the bottom of the waist. The long sleeve is finished at the hand with satin folds and loop trimming: the epaulette is a mixture of satin and *soie de Londres*, disposed in an extremely novel and tasteful style, for which we refer to our print. Falling collar, finished with bands of satin and loop trimming. Head-dress, a bonnet composed of white watered *gros de Naples*; the brim, of a moderate size, turns up a little, and is ornamented under the edge with a band of blue tufted gauze; a piece of *gros de Naples* goes round the crown, cut at bottom and top in the form of leaves, and edged with narrow straw plait. A full bunch of these leaves and a bouquet of *marguerites* are placed on one side of the crown, and a bouquet of *marguerites* only on the other. Broad white satin strings, tied in a full bow on the left side. Black kid shoes. Limeric gloves.

Evening Dress
August 1821

EVENING DRESS

A figured lace round dress over a white satin slip: the body is tight to the shape, and the waist of the usual length; it is cut moderately low round the bust, which is trimmed with an intermixture of folds of net and pink satin. Full sleeve, composed of lace over white satin, intermixed in a tasteful and novel manner with small bouquets of moss roses. At the bottom of the skirt is a full rouleau of pink satin wadded; this is surmounted by bouquets of leaves in pink satin, arranged at equal distances from each other, and between each is an ornament, in the form of a star, composed of five small roses. A rich satin sash, the middle white, the edges pink, tied in full bow and long ends behind, finishes the dress. The hair is arranged in light but full curls on the temples. Head-dress, a coronation hat, composed of *gaze de laine*. We refer for the form of this elegant hat to our print: it is finished at the edge with narrow pointed blond, and is ornamented with a diamond loop and a superb plume of white ostrich feathers, which droop a little to one side. Necklace, cross, ear-rings, and bracelets, diamonds. White kid gloves, finished with a full quilling of tulle. White satin slippers.

We are indebted to Miss Pier-point of No. 12, Edwards-street, Portman-square, inventress of the *corset à la Grecque*, for both these dresses.

Walking Dress
September 1821

WALKING DRESS

A black bombasine high gown; the body is made tight to the shape; the collar, which falls in the pelerine style, is covered with folds of black crape, placed one above another. The long sleeve is rather tight, and is finished at the hand with folds to correspond. The epaulette is very full; it is composed of crape; the fullness is intersected by narrow bands composed of plaited crape, terminated at the bottom by small rosettes. The trimming of the bottom of the skirt consists of a number of folds cut bias, and placed one above another. The pelisse worn over this dress is of black *gros de Naples;* the body tight to the shape, and the bust finished in front with black crape braiding. The sleeve is of an easy width; it is adorned at the hand by a broad band of black crape, with a full rouleau at each edge. The epaulette consists of large puffs of crape, something in the crescent form, drawn through bands of silk. High standing collar, covered with crape. The bows which fasten the pelisse up the front are also of crape; they are very full, with pointed ends. The trimming of the bottom of the skirt, for the form of which we refer to our print, is likewise of the same pointed at top: black crape flower, and *gros de Naples* strings. The cornette worn under the bonnet is of white crape, as is also the ruff. Black chamois shoes and gloves.

Evening Dress
September 1821

EVENING DRESS

A low gown made of a new material, black crape figured with black satin; it is worn over a black sarsnet slip: the *corsage* is cut square, and low round the bust, which is decorated with a wreath of white crape leaves, and folds of the same material shade the bosom. The shape of the back is formed by a new brace of a singularly pretty make; it is in the figure of a heart behind, and finished at the bottom by a full crape bow: three bands, placed at some distance from each other, form the shape at the sides. Short full sleeve, confined to the arm by a crape band. The trimming of the skirt is composed of plain black crape intermixed with black *gros ds Naples*, and silk buttons; it is of a perfectly novel form, as will be seen by our print. The hair is dressed low, and in full but light ringlets at the sides of the face, and very far off the forehead. A wreath of black crape roses goes round the head. Necklace and ear-rings, jet. Black chamois leather shoes and gloves.

We are indebted to Miss Pierpoint of No. 12, Edwards-street, Portman-square, inventress of the *corset à la Grecque*, for both these dresses.

22

Walking Dress
October 1821

WALKING DRESS

A high dress, composed of *ponceau gros de Naples*; the *corsage* fastens behind; the back is plain; the fronts are ornamented by a trimming of the same material, in the form of a wreath of leaves, which slopes down on each side, and forms the shape of the bust in a very becoming manner. The collar is very deep, and is ornamented at the edge by a loop trimming. Long sleeve, finished at the hand by a loop trimming: very full epaulette, terminated by a band and bow in the middle of the arm in front; a similar bow surmounts the trimming of the bottom of the sleeve. There is a full *ruche*, of the same material as the dress, at the bottom of the skirt; this is surmounted by a trimming also of the same material, of an uncommonly novel and pretty description, for which we must refer to our print. Head-dress, a bonnet of *gros de Naples*, to correspond: it is of a moderate size, lined with white, and adorned with a very full plume of white feathers, tinged at the edge with the same colour as the dress; strings, to correspond, tie it under the chin. The hair is much divided on the forehead, and very full at the sides of the face. Necklace and earrings, dead gold. Limerick gloves, and black kid shoes.

Court Dress
October 1821

COURT DRESS

A white lace petticoat, of Urling's manufacture, over one of white satin; the trimming of the petticoat consists of gold tissue disposed in folds, and edged with gold cord; train of gold-coloured satin lined with white satin, and trimmed with bunches of gold shells, placed at regular distances: this trimming goes all round. The *corsage* is tight to the shape; the front is formed of folds, to correspond with the trimming of the petticoat. Sleeves of gold-coloured satin, trimmed with folds of tissue and gold cord; a band of plaited cord terminates the sleeve. A very full Elizabeth ruff stands up round the back of the neck. The hair is divided so as to display the forehead very much; it falls in loose ringlets at the sides of the face. The hind hair is dressed low. A diamond bandeau is placed very low over the forehead; the lappets are of Urling's point lace: a profusion of white ostrich flat feathers finishes the *coeffure*. Diamond ear-rings and necklace. White kid gloves, and white satin shoes.

We are indebted to Miss Pierpoint of No. 12, Edwards-street, Portman-square, inventress of the *corset à la Grecque*, for both these dresses.

Promenade Dress
November 1821

PROMENADE DRESS

A pelisse, composed of dark violet-coloured velvet: the body is tight to the shape, rather long in the waist, and a good deal sloped at each side of the back. The sleeve is an easy width; it is terminated by a French cuff: the pelisse wraps across in front, and is trimmed with satin of the same colour: we refer for the form of this very novel and tasteful trimming to our print; and shall only observe, that the little bands which separate the heading from the bottom, are of velvet, and that the trimming goes all round the collar and cuffs, which are trimmed to correspond: the pelisse is lined with white sarsnet. A cachemire shawl is thrown over the shoulders, and fastened at the throat with a brooch. Lace ruff, made very full. Head-dress, a bonnet composed of violet-coloured velvet, and lined with white satin; the shape is very well adapted for walking: it is rather close, but becoming. The brim, of moderate size, turns up a little, and is finished just under and above the edge with bands of white *velours nalté*. A very full plume of violet-coloured ostrich feathers is placed on one side of the crown; the strings correspond. Boots of violet kid. Limerick gloves. Ermine muff.

Evening Dress
November 1821

EVENING DRESS

A round dress, composed of blond net over a white figured satin slip. The *corsage* is cut square round the bust, and is ornamented with a wreath of Provence roses. The sleeves, which are very short and full, are of blond over white satin; the fulness partially conceals the roses which form it into draperies. The bottom of the skirt is finished by a wreath of Provence roses placed near the edge. This is surmounted by a trimming of the same material as the dress: it is in folds; they are edged with white satin, and form cavities, placed at some distance from each other; a bouquet of roses is put in every cavity. This trimming is at once tasteful, simple, and novel, and the general effect of the dress is uncommonly beautiful. The hind hair is arranged in braids and bows, which do not rise much above the crown of the head. The front hair is brought very low at the sides of the face in light curls: the forehead is left bare, with the exception of a single ringlet in the middle. A coral wreath is placed rather far back. Necklace and ear-rings pearl. White kid gloves and white satin slippers.

We are indebted to Miss Pierpoint of No. 12, Edwards-street, Portman-square, inventress of the *corset à la Grecque*, for both these dresses.

Promenade Dress
December 1821

PROMENADE DRESS

A dark lavender poplin high dress, with a plain tight body; full epaulette; the fulness confined by two large leaves, which are crossed in the middle of the arm; they are composed of *gros de Naples*: the sleeve is rather tight; it is finished at the hand by a chain trimming of plaited *gros de Naples*. The trimming of the bottom of the skirt consists of a fulness of this latter material, which is formed into lozenge puffs by poplin points, corded with *gros de Naples*, and fastened down by small silk ornaments. The pelisse worn over this dress is of turtle-green cachemire, lined with white sarsnet and wadded: it is tied down the front by bows of the same material, each of which is ornamented with a small steel clasp in the centre. The body is tight to the figure; an embroidery of a novel description goes down the fronts, and forms the shape in a very graceful manner. High standing collar, also embroidered. Sleeve of an easy width, and terminated by a singularly pretty cuff, for which we refer to our print: tight epaulette, notched like the teeth of a saw. The *ceinture* is of the same material as the pelisse; it is very broad, and is fastened at the side by a steel clasp. Very full lace ruff. Head-dress, the *chapeau à la paysanne*, composed of black velvet, and lined with white zephyreene: the trimming is a mixture of these materials; there is a full bow, with a steel clasp in the middle, placed to one side, and a long full plume of black feathers. Black leather half-boots, lined with fur. Limerick gloves.

Full Dress
December 1821

FULL DRESS

A white velvet round gown; plain body, of a moderate length, finished by a blond tucker *à l'enfant.* A wreath of wild flowers goes from the point of the shoulder round the back. The under-sleeve is of white satin and very loose, but it is confined by another, composed of plaited bands of white velvet, terminated by a row of blond turned up in waves, and intermixed with flowers. The bottom of the skirt is trimmed with a deep embroidery in white silk: this is surmounted by a trimming of a new material, which forms a full *ruche,* and is twisted round a white satin rouleau. Head-dress, *en cheveux*: the hind hair is disposed in bows, which are intermingled with variegated laurel-leaves: the front hair is parted so as to leave the forehead nearly bare; it is dressed in loose ringlets, which fall very low at the sides of the face. White kid gloves; white *gros de Naples* slippers. Crape fan, embroidered in steel spangles.

We are indebted to Miss Pierpoint of No. 12, Edwards-street, Portman-square, inventress of the *corset à la Grecque,* for both these dresses.

Morning Dress
January 1822

MORNING DRESS

A high gown composed of bright rose-coloured levantine: the bottom of the skirt is trimmed with a broad *bouilloinné* of the same material, above which is a flounce edged with velvet to correspond, and disposed in a scroll pattern; there are two rows, each turned the same way, and a rouleau of levantine placed between. The body meets in front: it is ornamented with straps placed bias, and each finished with a Brandenbourg; the back is plain, and extremely narrow at the bottom. Spring collar, trimmed with a full fall of the same material. Sleeve moderately wide; cuff cut in three points, finished by Brandenbourgs. The epaulette, for which we must refer to our print, is extremely novel and pretty. Head-dress, a *demi- cornette* composed of Urling's lace; the caul is something higher than they have been lately worn; narrow border, made very full: a bouquet of roses is placed rather far back. The hair is parted so as to display almost the whole of the forehead, and is dressed lightly at the sides. Black kid shoes. Limerick gloves.

Full Dress
January 1822

FULL DRESS

A white satin round gown; the bottom of the skirt is trimmed in a very novel style with blond intermixed with white satin. The *corsage* is cut low and square; the bust is edged with a plaiting of satin, and the lower part of it is ornamented in front with satin edged with narrow blond, and disposed in a scroll pattern. The sleeve is a mixture of blond and white satin; the former full, and confined by lozenges of the latter, the point of each finished by a Provence rose: the bottom of the sleeve is confined by a band to correspond. White satin sash, embroidered at each end in a bouquet of roses, and tied in full bows and long ends. Head-dress, *encheveux*. The front hair is parted to display the forehead, and falls very low at the sides of the face in light loose ringlets. The hind hair is disposed in plaits, through which a wreath of Provence roses is carelessly twisted. Ear-rings and necklace diamonds: the latter is a *negligé*. White kid gloves, and white *gros de Naples* slippers.

We are indebted to Miss Pierpoint of No. 12, Edwards-street, Portinan-square, inventress of the *corset à la Grecque*, for both these dresses.

Head Dresses
February 1822

HEAD DRESSES

No. 1. A Black velvet bonnet, lined with that sort of silk plush which the French call Cupid's wings; the ground is rose colour; the long curled silk which forms the pile is of lavender. The brim is of a moderate size, finished at the edge by bands of black satin. The bottom of the crown is also ornamented with satin bands, which terminate in a full star placed on one side, and clasped in the middle with a steel ornament; the top of the crown is ornamented en *marmotte* with velvet slashed in the Spanish style, and the spaces filled with *ponceau* ribbon, embroidered with black at the edges; it passes under the chin, ties in a full bow at the right side, and a long round black feather falls very low on the left.

No. 2. A dress hat, composed of black velvet and gauze; the latter disposed in full folds, and confined by steel ornaments: the brim is extremely small; it is formed of folds of gauze laid over velvet: a full plume of round black feathers is placed in front.

No. 3. A turban, composed of silver gauze intermixed with blue silk net: it is ornamented with full rosettes at each side; a drapery of blue net, corded with silver gauze, goes across the back part of the crown. The lower part of the turban is composed of bands of silver gauze slightly corded with blue satin.

No. 4. Turban *à la Ninon*, made of *tulle*, embroidered in steel. The material is disposed in full folds in front, and plumes of white marabouts placed between.

No. 5. A half-dress *cornette*, composed of Brussels point: the caul is rather high; the ears are broad, as is also the double border, which is very full. A rosette of Urling's lace, and a bow of blue and white ribbon, ornament the caul; plain blue strings.

Full Dress
February 1822

FULL DRESS

A round dress composed of black velvet; the skirt is something narrower than they have lately been worn, particularly at top, and the fulness is thrown entirely into the middle of the back. The bottom of the skirt is slightly scalloped; the scollops edged with a row of Urling's point laid on with a little fulness; above this is a trimming *en rosaces* composed of white satin with pearl hearts; a wave lightly embroidered in pearls surmounts this trimming. The *corsage* is cut low round the bust, tight to the shape, and the waist of the usual length. The bust is ornamented in front with white satin *creves*, finished by pearl tassels. A row of point lace, to correspond with the bottom, goes round the bust: it is single in front, and moderately full, but doubled round the shoulders and back, and has the effect of an epaulette; it is surmounted by a pearl trimming in the form of a chain. Short full sleeve, ornamented with white satin *creves* to correspond with the bust, and terminated with a plain band of black velvet, also adorned with pearls. The hind hair is disposed in Grecian plaits, which are wound round the head; the front hair is arranged in light ringlets brought low at the sides of the face. Head-dress, white ostrich feathers. Necklace and ear-rings, pearl. White kid gloves. White *gros de Naples* sandals.

We are indebted to Miss Pierpoint of No. 12, Edwards-street, Portman - square, inventress of the *corset à la Grecque*, for these dresses.

Promenade Dress
March 1822

PROMENADE DRESS.

A poplin high gown, made tight to the shape: the collar is very deep; it falls over, and is finished at the edge by a satin trimming, resembling shell-work: the long sleeve is rather tight to the arm; the epaulette is loose and shallow, and is finished at the edge to correspond with the collar; the bottom of the long sleeve has also a similar trimming: the skirt is moderately wide, and less gored than they have lately been worn; it is trimmed at the bottom with three deep flounces, placed near each other, disposed in the drapery style, and headed by a wreath of shell-work in satin, to correspond with the *corsage*. The pelisse worn over this dress is composed of dove-coloured lutestring, lined with rose-coloured sarsnet, and wadded: the fulness of the skirt is thrown very much behind; a broad band of ermine goes round the bottom, and an extremely novel trimming, for which we refer to our print, goes up the fronts: the back is tight to the shape; the collar falls over in the pelerine style; the long sleeve is finished at the hand with ermine. Slashed epaulette, with satin folds drawn across the slashes. Head-dress, a bonnet of a new cottage shape of rose-coloured lutestring, turned up in front: a bouquet of Provence roses goes round the crown: rose-coloured strings. Very full lace ruff. Black shoes and Limerick gloves.

Full Dress
March 1822

FULL DRESS

A white satin gown, cut low and square round the bust; the *corsage* is fastened behind, and draws in with a little fulness at the waist. The front of the bust is composed of alternate bands of white satin and Urling's lace, which forms the shape in a very new and graceful manner: the upper part of the bust is cut round in points, and these points form a narrow blond tucker into plaits. The sleeve is of white lace intermixed with satin: a row of deep points, composed of the latter material, goes round the top of the shoulder, in the epaulette style; the lace is disposed in *creves*, each of which is ornamented in the middle with a full how and ends of satin. The trimming of the skirt consists of a deep fold of satin at the bottom: it is wadded, and surmounted by a net *bouillonné*, interspersed with narrow satin rouleaus disposed in chains, each connected by bows, and finished by bouquets of heath-blossoms of different colours. Head-dress, a blond net hat: the front of the brim is cut in scollops, and turned up: round crown, of a moderate size; the net is disposed over it in a little fulness, and spotted with gold beads; the top is embroidered in white silk and *chenille*, intermixed with gold beads: the front of the crown is adorned with short full plumes of marabouts, with a bouquet of heath-blossoms between each. Neck -lace and ear-rings pearl. White kid gloves. White satin shoes.

Promenade Dress
April 1822

PROMENADE DRESS

A French gray poplin round gown, made to fasten behind; the bust is ornamented on each side with *chenille* to correspond, in a scroll pattern, in such a manner as to form a stomacher *à l' antique*. Long tight sleeve, with a full epaulette, consisting of two falls disposed in bias, and stiffened at the edges, so as to stand out from the long sleeve: they are lightly embroidered at the edge in chenille. The bottom of the long sleeve is pointed, and finished at the edge with *chenille*. The trimming of the skirt consists of a rouleau of *gros de Naples* to correspond at the bottom, surmounted by a trimming of *gros de Naples*, quilled in the middle, and set on in a serpentine direction. The pelisse worn over this dress is composed of a colour between a peach-blossom and a red lilac lutestring; it meets in front, and is tied up with bows of bound lutestring. The bottom of the skirt is finished by a broad band of velvet to correspond, with branches of leaves issuing from it, disposed in a scroll pattern, and bound with lutestring. The body is ornamented on each side of the bust with French folds, finished at one end by a rosette of crimped cord, and at the other by a bullion frog. The back is tight, and the hips are ornamented with frogs to correspond. Tight sleeve, finished at the hand in a rich pattern of lutestring leaves edged with satin. Full epaulette, slashed across in an oval form, and the middle of each slash ornamented with lutestring leaves. Head-dress, a bonnet of white figured gros de Naples, trimmed with amber gauze, disposed in drapery folds across the back of the crown, and brought round to the bottom of the crown in front: the edge of the brim is finished by narrow folds of ponceau and amber satin. A full hunch of flowers adorns the crown, and white *gros de Naples* strings tie in a full bow on one side. Black shoes. Limerick gloves.

Evening Dress
April 1822

EVENING DRESS

The evening dress is composed of gray silk; the trimming of the skirt is of net, laid on full, and divided into compartments by narrow satin rouleaus, terminating at the top in points, each point finished by three white satin leaves; a double rouleau of white satin goes round the edge of the bottom of the skirt. The *corsage* is of net; it is full on each side of the bust, the fulness confined in the middle by a narrow band of satin; it is sloped down at each side to form the shape of the bosom, and is edged by a singularly pretty satin trimming, which also goes round the bust. The *corsage* is cut low and square round the bust; the waist is of the usual length; a netsash, richly wrought in steel, is tied on one side. Short full sleeve, composed of Urling's net, finished at the bottom by a narrow satin band, and ornamented with satin in the form of bats' wings. Hair dressed low behind, full on the temples, and less divided on the forehead than usual. Head-dress, a double wreath of spring flowers. Necklace and ear-rings, pearl. White kid gloves. White *gros de Naples* slippers.

Morning Dress
May 1822

MORNING DRESS

A round dress, composed of *batiste*: the bottom of the skirt is embroidered in a running pattern of *pensées* in yellow silk, surmounted by a wreath of the same flower disposed in a wave. High body, to fasten behind, and with a little fulness at the bottom of the back: the bust is plain, and is cut moderately high on the shoulder; the waist the usual length. Long sleeve, very tight, and finished by a pointed cuff; the points turn upwards, and are edged with yellow satin. Full epaulette, cut in slashes, which are filled with satin, to correspond with the trimming. A very full ruff, composed of Urling's lace, completely envelopes the throat. The head-dress is a *demi-cornette*, made of blond *monti*, and trimmed with yellow gauze ribbon: the form, for which we refer to our print, is remarkably simple and elegant. Black kid shoes, and gloves to correspond with the trimming of the dress.

Full Dress
May 1822

FULL DRESS

Round dress, composed of *tulle*, over a white satin slip: the bottom of the skirt is finished by a garniture of *tulle* intermixed with pearls; this is surmounted by a trimming composed of *tulle*, *chenille*, and pearls, disposed in alternate wreaths of corn-flowers and roses: this trimming has a striking and elegant effect. The *corsage* is cut low, and in such a manner as to give considerable width to the chest: it is tight to the shape. Three falls of *tourterelle* points go entirely round the bust. Sleeve composed of tulle over white satin; it is short and full, and ornamented with points to correspond. The front hair is dressed in light full ringlets, which fall very low at the sides of the face. The hind hair is arranged in bows somewhat higher than it has lately been worn. Head-dress, a very full plume of white ostrich feathers, and a pearl sprig. Necklace and ear-rings, pearl. White kid gloves, and white *gros de Naples* shoes.

We are this month indebted to Miss Pierpoint of No. 12, Edward-street, Portman-square, inventress of the *corset a la Grecque,* for both our dresses.

Court Dress
June 1822

COURT DRESS

The gown is composed of a new and very beautiful white transparent material: it is worn over a white satin slip, and is finished at the bottom of the skirt by a trimming which may be styled a net- work of puffs; they are composed of *tulle*, crossed with pink gimp, and divided by moss rose-buds. The trimming consists of three rows: the effect is very striking. The *corsage* is cut low; it is rounded at the bust, which is shaded by a blond tucker: the lower part of the bust is ornamented with pink satin cheviornels, edged with blond. Short full sleeve, decorated with blond and rose-buds to correspond. The train is composed of pink watered lutestring, trimmed round with a *bonillonné* of *tulle*, which is divided into small compartments by moss rose-buds. The front hair is arranged in light loose curls at each side, so as to leave the forehead a good deal exposed. Head-dress, diamonds, and a profusion of white uncurled ostrich feathers. Necklace and earrings, diamonds. White kid gloves, and white satin shoes.

Evening Dress
June 1822

EVENING DRESS

A round gown, composed of *buf crepé lisse*: the skirt is ornamented with a trimming of the same material, intermixed with leaves formed of blue satin and *gros de Naples*, disposed in two rows of stars, irregularly placed. Beneath this trimming is another, composed of bands of the same material, with satin *créves* let in. The *corsage* is tight to the shape; the waist is rather more than the usual length, and the bust is cut low: it is rounded in front, and ornamented at top with a wreath embroidered in blue silk. Short sleeve, formed in the Spanish style, with full puffs and spaces between, embroidered in blue to correspond with the *corsage*. The hind hair is brought rather high, and arranged in full bows. The front hair is a good deal divided, and dressed low at the sides. Head-dress, a bouquet of wild flowers. Necklace and ear-rings, pearl. Blue kid shoes, and white kid gloves.

We are indebted for this dress to Miss Pierpoint, inventress of the corset a la Grecqne, of No. 12, Edward-street, Portman -square.

Morning Dress
July 1822

MORNING DRESS

The morning dress is composed of colonnade stripe muslin, worked round the bottom to correspond with the stripe, and trimmed with four narrow worked flounces, the upper one finished with a double row of cord. The body fastens behind, plain and high, but a little open towards the throat; trimmed with the same delicate work that decorates the cape, in which there are two rows, separated by a puffing of plain book-muslin, through which a lilac ribbon is drawn. The cape is square at the shoulder, where it finishes; but the upper row of trimming is continued to the bottom of the waist, adding to the gracefulness of the form. The sleeve is worked at the end, and tied with lilac ribbon at the wrist; above which, the work is arranged in a double angle trimmed, from each of which is suspended a small cord tassel. The cap is elegantly simple, of the cottage form, and composed of beautiful India worked and Mechlin lace, tastefully decorated with fancy lilac ribbon. Shoes, lilac kid.

41

Evening Dress
July 1822

EVENING DRESS

Round dress, of delicately striped net, over a white satin slip; the bottom of the dress extended by a double rouleau of rich white satin; above which are elegant festoons, arranged transversely, of puffed *crépe lisse*, confined diagonally by three narrow rouleaus of white satin, and finished at the top with small clusters of the blue convolvolus. The *corsage* displays the chastest taste, cut round, and edged with a quilting of the finest *tulle*; the stomacher is formed of four rows of six minute folds of white satin, net appearing between each row. The tasteful trimming round the back, over the shoulder, and uniting with the stomacher to the bottom of the waist, is composed of short rows of folded satin, separated by the net at equal distances, and edged with blond, of a rich and elegant pattern. The sleeve short and full, confined by convolvoluses and divisions of small folded satin, which is again intersected by cheveronels. — Head-dress, turban of cerulean blue and white *crépe lisse*, and two white ostrich feathers. The hair parted in front, and elegant ringlets on each side. White satin shoes, long white kid gloves. Necklace and ear-rings of pearl and cornelian.

42

Walking Dress
August 1822

WALKING DRESS

A SILK pelisse, of a beautiful pale Spanish green, made to fit the shape; long sleeve, easy, but not tight; full epaulette, confined with three bands, the lower half of each embroidered and edged with satin of the same colour. The buttons which unite the front are concealed, and are on the inside. The side is ornamental with a new and elegant calyx trimming in satin: a broad plain rouleau of satin gives effect and finish to the bottom of the skirt. A rich worked vandyke collar falls over the plain low one of the pelisse. Granadine scarf of rose colour. Cottage bonnet of *gaze métallique*, decorated with leaves of the same light material, and *roses à cent feuilles*. Bonnet caps, with a full border of Northamptonshire lace. Jonquil kid gloves and boots.

Evening Dress
August 1822

EVENING DRESS

A round dress, of fine tulle, ornamented with rich colonnades of folded white satin, narrow at the wrist, and slightly extending to their termination, with a star composed of a centre rose, green leaves, and leaves *en applique*; beneath are *chevrons* of roses, leaves, and May blossoms; three rouleaus of white satin, the upper one entwined with rich pink satin, harmonizing with elegant simplicity the colour and form of this tasteful decoration. The stomacher of white satin and tulle: the bosom shaded with a tucker of delicate blond. Short sleeve of tulle, interspersed with small rouleaus of satin and blond. Head-dress, a *toque* of tulle and white satin; two rows of pearl are continued all round, above which a twisted rouleau of satin confined by pearls gives richness, and a light ornamental trimming decorates the front: it is edged with four rouleaus, and finished with blond, continued in flutes to the side, where it terminates *en serpent* with pearls: white satin crown. The colour of the feathers accords with the dress; they are placed on one side, and appear through the tulle, and fall over the opposite shoulder. Embroidered Persian crape scarf. — White kid gloves and white satin shoes. Ear-rings and necklace of rubies and pearl.

Ball Dress
September 1822

BALL DRESS

Dress of fine tulle over a white satin slip, ornamented nearly half the depth of the skirt with scollops of pink net and steel; the latter formed by a large steel button in the centre, and a semicircle of small steel beads. Short full sleeve, composed of alternate rows of pink net and steel, and white tulle and steel scollops, confined by a band of pink net and steel. Tucker, a quilling of the finest tulle. Sash of pink and white embroidered satin ribbon. A wreath of roses confines the hair, which is in ringlets, as in the reign of Charles II. and presented to our admiration in the beautiful paintings by Vandyke. Necklace, red cornelian and pearl. Gloves of white kid; shoes, white *gros de Naples*.

Court Dress
September 1822

COURT DRESS

This elegant robe and petticoat were made for a lady of high rank and taste, as a presentation dress at the palace of Holyrood. It is of pale blue silver lama, over a blue satin slip; thus combining Scotland's national colours of blue and white, now so prevalent among the leaders of *hunt ton*: the waist is of that graceful length which cultivated taste has adopted, and which we hope will long be retained. The stomacher is of silver vandykes: a double row extends over the shoulders and back, united by silver roses. The sleeve is short, and of novel construction, consisting of a dozen rows of silver vandyke trimming, separated by blue satin pipings, confined by a silver band round the arm, and finished with the same trimming. The tucker is fine blond lace. The robe and petticoat have an elegant border of large roses, of blue gofre crape and silver, half encircled with thistles, which form a kind of radii, giving lightness and effect to the trimming, which is edged with a silver wave, and finished with scolloped gofre crape. The head-dress is of diamonds, with a superb plume of ostrich-feathers. Neck-lace and ear-rings of diamonds and sapphires. White kid gloves; white satin shoes, with blue and silver roses.

Morning Dress
October 1822

MORNING DRESS

This elegant morning dress is of mull muslin; the body cut bias, and beautifully worked in small sprigs; a falling collar, with square corners, a little open in the front, and fastened with a pearl brooch, and trimmed all round with fine British lace. The trimming of the waist partakes of the stomacher and the jacket, it being deep, and pointed in the front with a worked star in the centre, but narrow as it approaches the sides. The sleeves are long, and trimmed at the top, and from the shoulder to the wrist, with small rosette-work, united by lozenges. The bosom and cuffs are finished with a single row of worked trimmings. The bottom of the skirt has a superb and novel trimming of rosettes of full or fluted work, with lace or open-work in the centre. The colour of the gloves, sash, shoes, and slip, is peach-blossom. The hair in ringlets, parted so as to display the forehead.

Evening Dress
October 1822

EVENING DRESS

The families of the ancient Scotch nobility were distinguished by their different plaids. That represented in the fashions for this month is the Mackenzie tartan, one of the most rich and varied in colour: it is of very rich silk. The *corsage* is made to fit the shape. The tucker is of *crépe lisse*, folded *à la Farinet*, confined in the front, on each side, and on the shoulders, by pearl loops. The sleeve short and full, set in a band of twisted satin, and edged with a delicate Buckinghamshire lace, ornamented with three circles of rich satin of the same colour as the dress, and united by rose-coloured knots; the band or girdle, ingeniously plaited of various coloured satins, harmonizing with the sleeve and trimming at the bottom of the skirt, which is of two flounces, composed of green net and narrow rouleaus of coloured satin, formed like Psyche's wings, and surmounted with a twisted rouleau of satin. Head-dress, plaited satin band, with an elegant pearl ornament in the centre; feathers, birds of Paradise. Necklace, ear-rings, and bracelets, of emerald and dead gold. Lilac satin shoes, with green and rose-coloured trimmings. Long white kid gloves. Chinese crape fan.

48

Walking Dress
November 1822

WALKING DRESS

This pelisse is made of silk, of a very delicate pattern, called by the French *peau de papillon*; its colour is a light shade of marguerite: the body is without any fulness, neat, close, and high; the collar is plain, and stands out to admit a large ruff. The upper sleeve is full, and slashed *à l' Espagnol*, confined half way of every division by *ailes de papillon*: the long sleeve almost fits the arm, and is finished by a garniture of *ailes de papillon*. Down the front of the pelisse is a plain piece of rich satin, of the same colour, cut bias, and continuing from the throat to the feet, gradually increasing in width, and on each side *ailes de papillon*, arranged form the points of chevrons: trimmings of the same kind, though reduced in size, is continued round the bottom of the pelisse. Bonnet, of white *gros de Naples*; the front edged with; twisted folds of white and cherry-coloured gauze; the flowers are a beautiful Scotch heath with red blossoms, and are tastefully intermingled with silk and gauze. — Boots, the colour of the pelisse; gloves, lemon colour. The hair parted, and a few light curls on temple; the hind hair twisted and fastened on the crown of the head *à l' antique*.

Evening Dress
November 1822

EVENING DRESS

Dress of fine tulle over an azure satin slip: the *corsage* is quite plain, and fastens behind; across the front, three rows of beautiful pearl beads supersede the tucker, and from thence over the shoulders and back falls a light and elegant lace: a band of satin and pearl confines the waist, and is fastened behind with a pearl clasp. Short full-dress sleeve, set in a band of satin and pearl; the fulness repressed by three chevrons of fluted net and satin; in the centre of each is a Gueldres rose and leaves of pearl. The bottom of the skirt is richly ornamented by festoons of lace, sustained by pearl loops; between each are Gueldres roses and leaves formed entirely of pearl: beneath this elegant device is a chaste simple wreath of pearl leaves *à l' antique*, surmounting a deep flounce of lace, which has small pearls attached to each flower. The forehead is displayed between the light and elegant curls that fall on each side; and a dress plume of white ostrich feathers, fastened to the hair behind and drooping forward, forms the head-dress. Necklace and ear-rings of pearl and sapphire. Long white kid gloves; azure satin shoes. Buff cashemire shawl.

We are indebted to Miss Pierpoint of No. 12, Edward-street, Portman-square, inventress of the *corset à la Grecque*, for this latter dress.

Carriage Morning Dress
December 1822

CARRIAGE MORNING DRESS

High dress of mulberry-coloured velvet, fastened behind. The collar is unornamented and projecting, and admits a full lace ruff. The long sleeve nearly fits the arm, and is finished with a pyramidal ornament of leaves, composed of velvet, edged with a double cord of *gros de Naples*: the base of the pyramid extends round the bottom of the sleeve, and confines it at the wrist. The epaulette consists of squares of velvet, edged with two rows of *gros de Naples* cord, and fastened at each point with knots of cord: across the bust, the pyramidal ornament is arranged longitudinally. Broad band of velvet edged with cord round the waist, and fastened behind with an elegant cut steel buckle. At the bottom of the skirt are three rows of chinchilla fur, equidistant, which harmonizes beautifully with the rich colour of the velvet. Long tippet and muff of chinchilla. Velvet bonnet, to correspond: the front at the edge is trimmed, within and without, with fluted velvet, and interspersed with wolves' teeth, or velvet points, edged with two rows of *gros de Naples* cord: the crown is low, and a folded *fichu* crosses it in part, and ties under the chin; a plumb of white ostrich feathers, fastened by a cluster of velvet points, surrounding a steer star, is placed on the right side of the bonnet, and falls gracefully towards the front. Bonnet cap of blond, with full border. Boots the same colour as the pelisse. Gloves citron colour.

Evening Dress
December 1822

EVENING DRESS

Dress of plain net over a gold coloured satin slip, lined throughout; the hem and two tucks wadded. The body of the dress is rather high, cut round, and edged with white satin: its fulness is horizontal, and regulated with perpendicular rouleaus of white satin, equidistant at the top, but approaching towards their termination at the waist, which is rather long, and confined by a white satin band, fastened behind with an elegant pearl clasp in the centre of a satin bow. Very full court sleeve of net, with satin rouleaus from the shoulder, set in a band round the arm. At the bottom of the skirt is a triple row of white satin *chevrons*, which are continued to a point nearly half a yard up the right side of the dress, and gradually descend behind, till they unite with those at the bottom. The head-dress is a garland of fancy flowers, interspersed with golden ears of corn; the hair in light and playful curls, a little parted in front. Necklace, ear-rings, and bracelets, of pearl and topaz. Long white kid gloves. White satin shoes, with gold trimming. Silk kerchief, or *élégantine*.

The chaste simplicity of these dresses displays the correct taste of Miss Pierpoint, who supplied both in the present Number [issue].

Morning Dress
January 1823

MORNING DRESS

Roman dress, or *blouse*, of fine cambric muslin: the body and skirt are in one, and of nearly equal fulness, which is principally collected in the front and in the middle of the back, and confined round the waist with a red narrow band, fastened by a steel buckle: it is made high, nearly to the throat, and is gaged with four rows of pink braiding. The sleeve is easy, and has an epaulette with full trimming, braided at the edge, and a double ruffle at the wrist: round the bottom of the skirt are five narrow flounces, edged with pink braiding. Cap of sprigged net, with border of British Lisle lace; cottage front; the caul rather full, and separated half-way into eight divisions, edged with a rouleau of satin: four, alternately, are fastened to the head -piece; the others are trimmed with lace, and rather elevated, forming a light and elegant crown: a wreath of delicate flowers, the forget-me-not and the heliotrope, decorate the front. Coral ear-rings, rose-coloured gloves, and corded silk shoes.
This cap and dress are from Miss Pierpoint.

Ball Dress
January 1823

BALL DRESS

White *crépe lisse* dress, worn over a bright pink satin slip; the *corsage* of white satin, cut bias, and fits the shape: it is ornamented with simple elegance, being separated into narrow straps, nearly two inches deep, and edged with two small folds of pink *crépe lisse* set in a narrow band of folded white satin, finished with a tucker of the finest blond lace. The sleeve is short, of very full white *creée lisse*, partly concealed by two rows of white satin diamonds, edged with pink *crépe lisse*, and united by half a dozen minute folds of white satin: at the bottom of the dress is one row of large full puffs, or *bouffantes*, of white *crepe lisse*; between each are eight white satin loops, attached to the *bouffantes*, and surrounding a cluster of half-blown China roses. The hair, without ornament, *à la Grecque*. Ear-rings, necklace, armlets, and bracelets, of dead gold, with pink topazes and emeralds interspersed, and fastened by padlock-snaps studded with emeralds. Long white kid gloves. Pink satin shoes.

Evening Dress
February 1823

EVENING DRESS

Pomegranate-colour *crépe lisse* dress; corsage to fit. The stomacher is composed of double rouleaus of satin, rather more than an inch apart, and is continued over the shoulder to the bottom of the waist behind, and is trimmed with fine blond, the same as the tucker. The band, or sash, is of *crépe lisse* edged with satin, and the ends of the rosette trimmed with blond. The sleeve is formed of three rows of small festoons of *crépe lisse*, edged with satin and blond. The skirt is decorated with an elegant net-work of pomegranate and white chenille, surmounted with a row of steel beads; a steel bead is introduced at each angle of the net: beneath is a tasteful trimming of *crépe lisse* in double reversed plaitings, intersected with ornamented semicircles of satin, united by a circlet composed of four satin rouleaus, with a row of small steel beads between each; a broad satin rouleau at the bottom of the dress. The hair in very full curls, and a garland of deep and pale coloured roses. Ruby neck-lace, armlet, bracelets, and ear-rings. Long white kid gloves, and white satin shoes. Opera cloak of rich black satin, wadded, and lined with cerulean blue sarsnet, edged with a small rouleau of blue satin: it is made very long, and with arm-holes: plain collar and large hood, which draws with blue ribbon.

Head-Dress
February 1823

HEAD-DRESSES

1. Bolivar hat of black velvet; the brim, narrow and of equal width, is continued from the right side above the satin band of the crown, forming a double front, which is finished on the left with a small gold tassel: the centre is pointed and tasselled: small gold beads entwine the edge, and form an elegant spiral ornament. On the left side is placed a *panache noir* Aladdin, which falls gracefully to the right.

2. Cap of *tulle*; the crown covered with throe satin tulip-leaves, edged with a small rouleau and double *crépe lisse* and blond, beginning with a satin bow on the left side; between each leaf is generally introduced a demi-wreath of fancy flowers of a ruby or cherry colour. Our print has a convolvolus in the front, which is of the cottage shape, bound with satin: French folds of satin head the border, which is of blond, and double in the front.

3. Circassian turban of silver muslin, with a bird of Paradise, beneath which is a rich ostrich feather falling very low on the left side.

4. Bonnet of *ponceau* velvet; round the front is a rouleau of *gros de Naples*, of the same colour; the velvet trimming is also edged with *gros de Naples*, and interspersed with variegated roses. This bonnet is very fashionable in black velvet and satin, with pomegranate-blossoms.

5. Bonnet composed of *gros de Naples* of two colours: the crown, which is round, and rather low, is of lemon colour; the front is of lavender colour, and very full, but confined by four flat straps, which are continued withinside, which is plain, and has a bunch of ranunculus on the right side. A high trimming, of lavender colour, nearly surrounds the crown, and is edged with a satin rouleau, as are also the three large puffs or *bouillons* in the front.

Walking Dress
March 1823

WALKING DRESS

A deep amethyst-colour silk pelisse of *gros de Naples*, wadded, and lined with pink sarsnet; a little wrapt, and fastened down the front with hooks and eyes: *corsage*, made plain and high, ornamented with *tasselled chevronelles*: circular projecting collar of velvet, of a deeper hue than the silk; two rows of velvet are placed down the front and round the bottom of the skirt: sleeve nearly to fit, with velvet cuff, and full epaulette, intersected with velvet straps. Ruff of Buckinghamshire lace; cap of the same, fastened under the chin with button and loop. Bonnet of the same silk as the pelisse, bound with broad velvet, and lined with pink satin: the front bent *à la Marie Stuart*; the crown surrounded with inverted conical rouleaus of velvet, equidistant, commencing with a silk knot: plume of ostrich feathers, of a bright amethyst colour, placed on the right side, and falling low on the left shoulder. Gloves the colour of the pelisse; corded silk boots, the colour of the velvet; and swansdown muff.

Evening Dress
March 1823

EVENING DRESS

Dress of *pink gros de Naples*: *corsage* to fit, edged with pink satin, and slashed to the form of the stomacher; the interstices, or scollops, are filled with pink gauze, connected by circlets, and forming a tasteful chain, which continues to the waist behind, and gives the shape of the back: full court sleeve, confined with straps, bound with satin, satin circlets fastening the ends: a band of satin and full trimming of fluted gauze finish the sleeve, which is of a moderate length. The skirt is decorated with a fanciful trimming of double gauze; each division of the puff *derobé* is supported by a satin rouleau, and the lower part projects as far again as the upper: sprigs of the *lonicera sempervirens*, or great trumpet honeysuckle, are disposed at regular distances above, and beneath is a satin rouleau; and the hem wadded. Broad pink satin sash, double bow and long ends. Blond lace scarf. Bracelets, ear-rings, and neck- lace of that beautiful stone, the pink topaz, set in embossed gold, to which a cross is generally suspended. Head-dress, a gold tiara, ornamented with brilliants. White kid gloves, and white satin shoes.

Morning Dress
April 1823

MORNING DRESS

High dress of Cyprus crape, of a pale lavender colour, fastened behind; from the throat, nine narrow bands of *gros de Naples*, bound with satin of the same colour, descend to the waist, confining the reversed plaiting that forms the front of the body; from the shoulder, on each side, is a triple wave of satin piping, with small satin leaves with corded edges: the long sleeve easy; neat cuff, with wave trimming and leaves: the upper sleeve is rather long and very full, with bands to correspond with the front: broad *gros de Naples* band, bound with satin round the waist, fastened behind with a steel buckle: three rows of minaret bells of *gros de Naples*, bound with satin, decorate the bottom of the dress, which is finished with a satin rouleau. Square collar of worked muslin, and worked muslin ruffles. Round cap of sprigged bobbinet, and a single border of British Lisle lace, set on with equal fulness all round, and trimmed with shaded gauze ribbon of azure and rose colour. Cachemire shawl, and jonquil-coloured gloves.

Evening Dress
April 1823

EVENING DRESS

Dress of white figured *gros de Naples;* frock front, without ornament, but rather full, and finished with a twisted rouleau of ethereal blue and white satin: the sleeve short and full, and set in a band of white satin: epaulette of white satin vandykes, bound with blue: the lower half of the sleeve is surrounded with a lozenge trimming of white satin bound with blue; the bottom of the skirt has five double rouleaus of blue and white satin, placed at equal distances, and is finished with a white satin rouleau: long sash of blue and white gauze ribbon: Sicilian scarf. The hair parted in front, with full curls on each side *à la Vandyke*, confined by two rows of pearl and a gold comb; a full plume of blue feathers, falling tastefully towards the front, and shading the left side of the face. Necklace, ear-rings, and bracelets, of pearl. Long white kid gloves, white satin shoes.

Walking Dress
May 1823

WALKING DRESS

Cloak or mantle of levantine silk, of *flamme de ponche* colour: at the bottom are four narrow satin rouleaus, and also round the hood, which is drawn with white satin ribbon: small square standing collar. The cloak is lined with white sarsnet, and for cool mornings and chilly evenings will be found appropriate and comfortable. The dress is of English twilled sarsnet, of pale primrose colour, made high: the body full, but drawn to fit the shape by several longitudinal rows, and fastens behind: the epaulette and cuff are full, and arranged *en bouffants* by the drawings: at the bottom of the skirt is a trimming of gauze, formed into *bouffants* by perpendicular satin straps. Leghorn bonnet, the year: pelisses, with a plume of white ostrich feathers fastened by a small bow of *flamme-de-ponche*.

Evening Dress
May 1823

EVENING DRESS

Dress of bright Spanish green tulle, trimmed with the same material and with satin, and worn over a satin slip of the same colour: the *corsage* is made plain, with a Farinet tucker of white *tulle*; the folds tastefully confined by six small rosettes of satin ribbon, equidistant, one being placed in the centre of the bosom, another at the back, and the remainder at the front and back of the shoulders; the band is of satin, and the waist is rather short: the sleeve is moderately long, and very full, and has four satin rouleaus, ornamented half way with a circlet of French folds, where the fulness of the sleeve is collected: at the bottom of the skirt is a very full trimming of *tulle*, in reversed plaitings, set in a satin frame; to the upper band are attached satin spikes, which extend rather more than half way, and give it a rich and lively appearance. The hair is divided in front, and confined by a garland of anemones; the hind hair plaited, and disposed *à la couronne*. Ear-rings, bracelets, and necklace, of topaz. White kid gloves, white satin shoes, and small ivory fan.

62

Carriage Dress
June 1823

CARRIAGE DRESS

High dress, of pale blue silk, fastened in front, and ornamented with a trimming of the same material, and edged with satin of the same colour: the trimming is flat, united, and broad in the centre, but separates and gradually diminishes; each division seems to be fastened by a silk button, and terminates in three points: the trimming is very broad at the bottom of the skirt, but lessens as it approaches the waist; it continues to the throat, and nearly covers the front of the *corsage*. The collar is square, and falls over, admitting a lace frill within; and the cape is rounded off to display the front. The long sleeve is nearly tight, and has a very free half-sleeve, set in a band rather narrower than that of the waist, and is ornamented to correspond with the bottom of the skirt, where rays, emanating from a point, form a semicircular trimming, which appears to rise from the satin rouleau that edges the dress. The ruff has a similar, though smaller trimming than the front; and the whole forms a neat and elegant dress, supplied by the taste of Miss Pierpoint; as is the cap, which is particularly light and novel, having the appearance of a coronet: it is made of tulle, and set in a white satin frame, with a wreath of Syria roses, and is generally worn at the back of the head, with the hair in very full curls, embossed gold ear-rings and chain, and circular eye-glass. Jonquil-colour gloves; blue corded silk shoes.

Ball Dress
June 1823

BALL DRESS

Dress of white *crépe lisse* over a white satin slip: the *corsage* is without fulness, and shaped *à la tunique*, narrow at the shoulder, but approaches so as to form a stomacher in front, which is simply ornamented with three bands, each consisting of two rows of satin piping, uniting with those that descend from the waist; two slope from the front, and are rounded off just above the *bouillonné* that decorates the bottom of the skirt: on each band is placed a cluster of roses, the highest being in the centre: the waist has a broad satin band, fastened behind with a gold buckle. Short full sleeve, tastefully confined by bands of double piping set in a broad band of satin and gold, and finished by a deep-vandyke of blond lace; bands of double piping head and finish the *bouillonné*, which is very full and broad, and divided transversely by satin bands. Gold tiara, embellished with rubies and turquoise, and a pendant pearl in the centre: the hair parted in front, with short light curls on the temple; the hind hair brought to the top of the head, and fastened by a bodkin of gold and turquoise. Necklace and ear-rings of turquoise. Long white kid gloves. White satin shoes. Painted ivory fan.

Morning Dress
July 1823

MORNING DRESS

Dress of plain jaconot muslin; the *corsage* made high, close to the shape, and fastened behind. The elegant fashion of ornamenting the front of the skirt has become very prevalent; that in our print has a pagoda trimming formed by bands edged with cord, and narrow trimming of work descending gradually and regularly till it reaches the bottom, where there are four narrow worked flounces, each headed by flat corded bands, the upper one surmounted by a row of delicate insertion-work, the same as is introduced on each side of the pagoda trimming. The *corsage* is nearly covered with similar bands, corded, trimmed and arranged on clear book muslin, narrow at the waist both in front and back, but extending the whole width on the shoulder: falling collar of worked muslin leaves; long sleeve, nearly tight; worked ruffle, and small pagoda trimming at the wrist, where it is tied with primrose-colour ribbon drawn through a narrow puffing of book muslin: the epaulette is divided in the centre, and tied at the top in a bow, and trimmed with a row of puffed book muslin and narrow work.

Ball Dress
July 1823

BALL DRESS

British tulle dress worn over a white satin slip: the *corsage* composed of white satin bands, branching from the front; each band corded and trimmed with narrow blond; two bands continue over the shoulder, and renew the same trimming at the back: the sleeve is of the melon form, with sprays of satin confining the tulle; in the centre is a circular space, occasioned b; the omission of the satin, and a cluster of China roses is introduced, which has a novel and elegant effect. The tucker is of fine blond, surmounting a satin band of French folds; from the wrist descends a succession of small oval baskets of tulle, edged with white satin, each containing a China rose and leaves: three rows of the same light tasteful baskets are continued round the bottom of the dress, white satin sash, with double how behind. Milanese head-dress, composed of thirteen pins, two stationary and one pendant ball; the pins are of gold, with the heads of patent pearl, and are stack circularly in a plaited band of the hind hair: this is a very pretty novel head-dress, and accords with the grace of feminine beauty and youthful fancy. Necklace, ear-rings, and bracelets, of embossed gold and pink topazes interspersed. White kid gloves, with a quilling of blond at the top; white satin shoes, and a rose-bud introduced in the centre of the white satin rosette.

Evening Dress
August 1823

EVENING DRESS

Dress of pink crape, ornamented with silk spots: the *corsage* is made plain and cut bias, and trimmed round the bust with triple leaves of watered *gros de Naples:* short full sleeve of corded bands, interwoven with similar leaves. The corsage and skirt are set in a corded band, and fasten behind. The skirt is trimmed with two rows of watered *gros de Naples*, separated into regular divisions at top and bottom, edged with cord, and drawn with a little fulness in the centre; a rouleau of watered *gros de Naples* at the bottom of the dress, which is from Miss Pieipoint. Ballasteros hat of tulle; the front is turned up, and edged with white satin and narrow blond, and ornamented with two satin rouleaus, about half an inch apart: on the left side the front is cut open and trimmed, which gives a light and pretty effect. The crown has a waved circular top, with three satin rouleaus waving round it: on the left side is a full plume of blue and white ostrich feathers, with a small plume of marabouts. Necklace, ear-rings, and bracelets, of pink topaz. White kid gloves, and white satin shoes sandalled.

Ball Dress
August 1823

BALL DRESS

Dress of blue tulle: the *corsage* round, and moderately high; full in the back and front, and confined round the bosom with a band of satin folds and tulle: beneath is a wreath composed of floss silk, satin, and blond. Short full sleeve of tulle, set in a corded band, and ornamented with floss silk leaves of the mountain ash, and triangular trimmings of satin edged with narrow blond: satin band with corded edges round the waist: the bow behind formed of small pointed leaves, corded and edged with blond. A wadded satin hem at the bottom of the skirt, which is made long, and indicates an inclination of resuming the train, which gives grace and elegance to the figure, and is particularly appropriate to full dress, except for the ballroom. Above the hem is an ornamented wave of floss silk, satin, and tulle, from which a branch or scroll rises, supporting three circular fancy flowers. Brussels lace scarf. The hair is dressed *à la Grecque*, but ornamented with Milanese pins of gold, with heads of imitative turquoise: on each side is a ball of the same, and a second pending from the left. Neck-lace and ear-rings of turquoise, set in embossed gold, and fastened by cameo snaps. White kid gloves, trimmed and tied at the elbow. Ivory fan, and white satin shoes.

Morning Dress
September 1823

MORNING DRESS

Lavender-colour dress of *gros de Naples* or lutestring, ornamented in front with a pinnatifid satin trimming of the same colour; narrow at the waist, and extending in width till it reaches the trimming at the bottom of the skirt, where it is placed longitudinally; beneath is a broad satin rouleau. The *corsage* is made three-quarters high, plain, with a satin band of French folds round the top, and fastens with hooks and eyes: corded satin *ceinture*, with a cluster of crescent-shaped points behind. Long sleeve, ornamented at the wrist with satin to correspond, and fastened with knots of folded satin: the epaulette is composed of two rows of crescent-shaped leaves: worked muslin ruffles, and muslin *chemisette*, with Spanish vandyke worked collar, fastened in front with a gold buckle. The hair parted on the forehead, and in large ringlets on each side, plaited, and bows of ribbon of the same colour at the back of the head. Ear-rings and necklace of amethysts. Bonnet of pink *crépe lisse*; the outside fluted, and edged with three rows of pearl straw, and finished with blond lace: round crown, confined by a band of French folds, and decorated with a quadrangular trimming, edged with pearl straw and blond; one point is placed in front, and ears of corn, heath and convolvulus, are fancifully intermixed.

Evening Dress
September 1823

EVENING DRESS

Dress of lemon-colour *crépe lisse*: the *corsage* made to fit the shape, and ornamented with five rouleaus of satin of the same colour; broad corded satin band round the waist: in front are seven corded rings or circlets, through which rise seven leaves, each composed of several small folds of satin, and terminated with a folded satin knot; palmated corded bow behind. Short full sleeve, crossed by satin French bands confined by knots into squares, and having *bouffants* of folded satin round the centre of the sleeve, which is finished with a corded satin band, edged with fine blond lace, the same as the tucker. The skirt is decorated with a satin corded diamond trimming, each diamond cut across, and a plaited *bouffant* introduced, concealing the division, and fastening the corner of the next diamond: broad satin hem at the bottom of the skirt. The hair is in full curls, and parted in front, confined by a wreath of anemones and convolvuluses, and mixed with small white marabouts in front and on the right side. Necklace, earrings, and bracelets of turquoise and amber. Lace scarf. White kid gloves and white satin shoes.

Morning Dress
October 1823

MORNING DRESS

High dress of mezereon green *gros de Naples*; made plain, and fastened behind; ornamented on each side of the bust with a corded satin trimming of double points, through the centre of which a plaited stem is interwoven: it nearly meets at the waist, but extends as it advances to the shoulders. Long sleeve, nearly tight, edged with satin, and ornamented at the wrist with a triplet of satin triangles crossed by folded circlets in the centre: full epaulette, separated into *bouffants* by satin ornaments: broad band, edged with satin, round the waist; and a rosette of corded leaves behind. Satin rouleau at the bottom of the skirt, and two rows of twisted satin cord above at equal distances: richly worked vandyke muslin ruff, and narrow worked ruffles.

Cap of white tulle or Paris net, bound with pink satin, having four borders of double *crépe lisse*, either twined one within the other, or else laid on in waves of alternate pink and white; straight in front, and full at the sides: the crown has a white satin corded ornament divided into five points; between the upper part of each is a puffing of net, and a white satin star, whose radii are composed of small folds, spreads over the top: clusters of roses and major convolvuluses are placed in the front and side. Jonquil-colour kid shoes.

Ball Dress
October 1823

BALL DRESS

Dress of pink lama gauze: the *corsage* plain, bound with pink satin, and ornamented at equal distances ·
with large pearls and a festoon of silver lace, supported in front with a diamond brooch. Bouquets of
Sicilian flowers are tastefully disposed on the bust and sleeves, which are short and very full, festooned
with silver lace, and set in a satin band round the arm: sash of the same material as the dress. The
petticoat has a very deep border of plaited tulle, confined at the top and bottom with a double rouleau
of pink satin, divided in the centre by a narrower; a branch of satin crosses, forming half-diamonds: at
the points are satin bows, and sometimes flowers are added.

Head-dress, a pearl band and tiara, fastened by bows of pearl on the left side: very little hair on the
forehead; and the hind hair is drawn high, and confined in a bunch by a cord of twisted pearl. Ear-rings,
necklace, and bracelets of pearl, with pink topaz snaps. White kid gloves and white satin shoes.

The above is from Miss Pierpoint.

Head-Dresses
November 1823

HEAD-DRESSES

1. Turban of blue *crépe lisse*, confined with white satin bands edged with blond, and ornamented with golden ears of corn.

2. Hair in short full curls on the forehead; ringlets on each side of the ear; a branch of Van Dieman's bells, or *campanule étrangére*, with stamens of spun glass, in front and at the top of the head: the hind hair drawn up plain, and supported by a gold comb.

3. Pale brown beaver riding-hat; silk band of the same colour, and a gold buckle in front. Brussels lace veil.

4. Fancy straw bonnet, lined with rose colour; a plume of white ostrich feathers tipped with rose colour on the right side, and a wreath of anemones and minor convolvuluses round the crown.

Full Dress
November 1823

FULL DRESS

Lace dress over a blue satin slip: the *corsage* full, supported in the centre by a row of white satin leaves formed into a stomacher in front, and shaped behind by blue satin lacings: very full sleeve, separated into *bouffants* by blue satin vandykes extending half way up the sleeve, and is finished by a broad vandyke lace: blue satin band, with radiated leaves behind. The skirt is elegantly ornamented with a row of white satin uniform flowers and an antique wreath of leaves in Moravian work, with a very rich embroidered border of flowers beneath, united by semicircular branches and roses to a pyramidal border that surrounds the bottom of the skirt. Tucker, of a double row of fine tulle: a small bouquet on the right side of the bust. The hair *à la Madonne* in front, with plaited bands round the head, and a bow at the back; demi-wreath of Persian roses behind. Ear-rings, necklace, and bracelets of dead gold. White kid gloves, trimmed *à la Fracalse*. Transparent painted horn fan. White satin shoes.

Full Dress
December 1823

FULL DRESS

Dress of bright poppy-colour India muslin, ornamented with small sprigs of gold. The *corsage* to fit, with an elegant stomacher, composed of double rows of gold lace, placed diagonally from the front and continued over the shoulder; the outside formed into vandykes: short full sleeve, incased in bands edged with gold; broad gold lace band round the waist; tucker of narrow blond. The skirt is decorated with gold lace, placed flat on the dress in perpendicular double columns of different height; the upper part finished with a wave, and the highest points terminated with three unilateral leaves of gold edged with very narrow blond; broad wadded hem at the bottom of the dress. Turban of gold and poppy-colour *crépe lisse*; the frame of alternate rows of the same coloured satins brought to a point in front, and satin bands of French folds supporting the large *bouffants* of *crépe lisse*: short coquelicot feather placed on the right side. Pearl ear-rings, bracelets, and necklace; blond lace scarf; French trimmed gloves, and white satin shoes.

Evening Dress
December 1823

EVENING DRESS

British lace dress: the waist rather long, and the *corsage* plain, with a Farinet tucker of fine tulle, tied in front by a bow of white satin ribbon: short full sleeve, set in a white satin band; perpendicular corded satin bands, ornamented halfway with bows of white satin ribbon, support the fulness of the sleeve: corded satin *ceinture*; rosette of corded leaves behind, with a highly wrought steel buckle in the centre. The skirt is trimmed with two flounces of deep blond lace, arranged in festoons; and a corded satin leaf, pointing downwards, unites three narrow satin pipings that head each flounce: a broad satin rouleau terminates the bottom of the dress. The hair is parted on the forehead, and in light curls round the face; hind hair disposed in bows at the top of the head, and a garland of flowers is placed rather back. Necklace of gold, with ornaments in front; ear-rings and bracelets to correspond. White kid gloves, and white satin shoes.

Morning Dress
January 1824

MORNING DRESS

Twilled sarsnet or levantine high dress, of a deep green colour, called by the French *eau de Nil*: the *corsage* fastens behind with hooks and eyes; is made to fit the shape, and ornamented with perpendicular wadded satin rouleaus of the same colour and equidistant: broad satin *ceinture*, with a uniform rosette behind. Long tight sleeve, edged with satin at the wrist, and fastened with a satin band, the outer part formed into a diamond, with a wadded knot in the centre. Short full upper sleeve, confined by satin rouleaus placed longitudinally, and supported with satin knots. The bottom of the dress has six wadded satin rouleaus, each headed with a narrow piping formed into waves or festoons, and supported with wadded satin knots; beneath is a broad satin hem: richly worked *collerette* and ruffles. *Bonnet de jolie femme* of British Mechlin lace; long strings of the same, trimmed with lace like the borders, which are drawn very full at the sides, where a bow of pink gauze ribbon is introduced beneath the cap, being of one piece of lace. The head-piece is formed by two drawings, and ties behind with pink satin ribbon: three separate bows or puffings of broad shaded pink gauze ribbon are placed in front. Embossed gold ear-rings, chain, and cross. Buff-colour Morocco shoes, tied with ribbon of the same colour.

Promenade Dress
January 1824

PROMENADE DRESS

Pelisse of levantine silk, or Terry velvet, of a rich brown colour (*couleur d'oreille d'ours*), made plain and high to fasten in front, with a neat standing collar, edged with satin of the same colour. The velvet (*velours épingle*), which promises to be very fashionable this winter, has not been worn for many years: it looks like very narrow cords, and forms elegant trimmings for silk pelisses: the *ceinture*, which fastens with a gold buckle in front, and the leaves and knots of the trimming, are made of it. The trimming is scolloped, and edged with satin, having a pair of leaflets introduced at each point through a slit, which is bound with satin, and reunited with a velvet knot behind the leaves. The *corsage* is ornamented from the shoulder to the waist, where the trimming approximates, and widens again in descending, till it reaches the ermine which goes round the bottom of the pelisse, and is a quarter of a yard in depth. The long sleeve has a full epaulette, ornamented with leaves, and the wrist is trimmed to correspond. Bonnet of the same material as the pelisse, lined with the same, and the inside edged with shaded velvet, rather more than an inch broad: the front *à la Marie Stuart*; the crown round, and rather low, ornamented with velvet flowers and bows of shaded velvet. Bonnet cap of Honiton, with very full borders fastening under the chin. Full lace ruff and ruffles. Terry velvet boots, the colour of the pelisse. Pale yellow gloves, and a shell reticule, with silver chain.

Walking Dress
February 1824

WALKING DRESS

A rich brown-colour cloth coat, made plain, and trimmed in front, where it fastens with graduated scollops of French braiding; broad at the shoulders, and lessening towards the waist, from thence extending till it reaches the bottom of the skirt, and finished on the outside with fringe of the same colour. Broad band of braiding round the collar, waist, cuffs, the bottom of the skirt, and the seams of the back, which meet in a point, and are ornamented in the centre, and finished with frogs. The epaulette is formed by a double row of fringe, and from the wrist an ornamented scroll of braiding extends half way up the arm. Black velvet bonnet, lined with the same; the brim very broad, and edged with amber colour satin and cord: the crown deep, and small towards the top; the velvet in large folds round it, and relieved with bands of amber-colour satin, garland of fancy flowers, and satin bands of French folds. Cottage cap, with full border of British Mechlin lace. Yellow gloves, chinchilla muff, and black satin boots.

Evening Dress
February 1824

EVENING DRESS

Dress of Urling's lace over a pink satin slip: the corsage *à la Rubens*; the front formed of four pink satin straps edged with white satin, and fastened on each side with small gold buckles. The sleeve short, and composed of four rows of pink satin squares edged with white; between each row a full puffing of lace appears: satin band round the arm. The angular-embroidered stripes of the skirt are terminated in festoons of flowers, and a deep flounce of scolloped lace arranged beneath, and the whole finished by a rich embroidered scolloped border: the length of the skirt approaches to a train. Spanish hat of pink satin, turned up all round, rather broad in front, where' it is slashed transversely, and *tulle* introduced, excepting towards the left side, where a feather protrudes, of which there is a full plume of pink and white. The crown has a quadrangular ornament, which is lined, and each corner turned over.
Ear-rings and bracelets of pearl set in gold; gold chain and cross. Long white kid gloves, lace scarf, and white satin shoes.

Morning Dress
March 1824

MORNING DRESS

Shaded striped silk dress of *gros de Naples*; the *corsage à la blouse*; the fulness confined at the top with three satin rouleaus, equidistant. Long easy sleeve, finished at the wrist with rouleaus of purple and aurora, or orange colour; the upper sleeve very full, and intersected with satin rouleaus, as at the wrist. The skirt touches the ground behind, and is finished with two satin rouleaus, of the darkest shades of each colour; above is an ornamented crescent, composed of three semicircular bands; the points or horns united by a satin star, and placed alternately up and down. Elizabethan ruff very fine tulle, worked muslin ruffles, *cornette* or cottage cap of *tulle*; border of double tulle, disposed in *bouffants* by alternate rouleaus of aurora and purple satin; one side has a double row of *bouffants* and a quilling of tulle behind: the strings are of broad figured gauze ribbon, cross under the chin, and tie at the top in the front of the cap. The hair parted in front, with a few ringlets on each side. Green cachemire shawl, and green kid shoes.

Evening Dress
March 1824

EVENING DRESS

Dress of yellow China crape; the *corsage* cut bias, made rather high and plain, simply ornamented round the bust with a wheel trimming of the same colour in satin and gauze, composed of ornamented rings placed at equal distances on a circular satin wadded stem or rouleau. The *corsage* is rather long, and set in a band with satin corded edges, and fastened behind with a rosette to correspond. Tucker of fine blond, drawn at top with a silken thread. Short full sleeve, with perpendicular rows of wheel trimming. The skirt is decorated with the same trimming, only much larger, and, with the wadded satin hem at the bottom, gives weight and grace to the folds of the drapery. The hair is arranged in one row of large regular curls; and two long yellow ostrich feathers, tipped with *ponceau*, are placed on the right side, and bend over the head. Necklace, ear-rings, and bracelets of topaz and turquoise. Embroidered lace scarf with Vandyke ends; white kid gloves; white satin shoes.

Dinner Dress
April 1824

DINNER DRESS

Dress of emerald green *gros de Naples*; *corsage* plain, and bordered at the top with a satin band of the same colour, and a narrow tucker of tulle: the sleeve is very short and full, and composed of *crépe lisse*; the fulness regulated by pyramidal bands of *gros de Naples*, and finished in a double satin band round the arm. A very novel kind of flounce ornaments the bottom of the skirt, which is cut nearly a quarter of a yard up, and a fulness of *crépe lisse* introduced, and formed into a regular row of demi-bells, the lower part kept extended by two satin pipings, and the top of each surmounted with a double satin circlet and a triplet of satin leaves appliquée. *Fichu of crépe lisse*, edged with satin piping, and trimmed all round with narrow blond, confined at the shoulders with corded leaves, and arranged in front to form a stomacher, the points coming below the *ceinture*, which is also edged with satin and blond, and unites behind in a leaf rosette with the corner of the fichu. The hair is separated in front, and a pearl comb confines it on each side from the temple; round the back of the head it is arranged in large regular curls. Ear-rings and necklace of rubies. White kid gloves; white satin shoes; India shawl.

Ball Dress
April 1824

BALL DRESS

Dress of pale pink tulle over a satin slip; the *corsage* rather long and full, of a moderate height; the bust is encircled with a row of pink satin leaves, uniformly arranged, and interwoven with a white satin rouleau: tucker of the finest blond: the sleeves are short and full, slashed and regulated by the entwining of a pink satin rouleau round the centre, and set in a folded band round the arm. The skirt has the novelty of a little fulness at the sides; and from the centre of the waist downwards is a satin trimming, cut transversely into oblong parallel segments, imperceptibly increasing in width till it reaches that which goes round the bottom of the skirt, which is of a regular size, and entwined by a white satin rouleau: beneath are two broad pink satin rouleaus. Head-dress, a wreath of Calamata blossoms or Provence roses; the hair parted on the forehead, in large curls on each side, and turned up behind *à la Grecque*. Necklace and ear-rings of pearl set in embossed gold, with an elegant cross of St. Louis in front. White kid gloves, and white satin shoes.

Morning Dress
May 1824

MORNING DRESS

Dress of jaconot muslin: the *corsage* made high and very full; the fulness longitudinally and regularly arranged by five bands, each formed of four or five small cords or bobbins, and edged on each side with narrow work: two of the bands terminate at the arm; the next widen from the centre of the waist, and extend over the shoulder, where they turn and meet about half way down the back. The sleeve is of an easy fulness: the epaulette slashed, and interlaced with amber-colour ribbon; between is a row of quadrangular *bouffants*. The cuff is neatly trimmed with a bobbined band and worked ruffle, and an ornament to correspond with the trimming of the skirt, which has a deep wreath of a fanciful and novel form, apparently confined to the dress by entwining an amber -colour ribbon, which forms the lower part into triangles: the upper becomes more pointed, and extends transversely about a quarter of a yard: the whole is corded, and trimmed with narrow work. Worked muslin ruff to correspond, drawn with gauze ribbon. Cap of sprigged net; the border of Buckinghamshire lace, set on plain in front, and a little full round the slashes of the cap, which are two on each side, where bows of amber and lilac gauze ribbon are introduced. The crown is circular, and ornamented with a narrow rouleau of amber satin and lace. Amber-colour corded silk shoes.

Dinner Dress
May 1824

DINNER DRESS

Dress of pale blue twilled sarsnet: the *corsage* cut bias, and made to fit the shape: the front simply ornamented with four satin bands, forming a stomacher, and a satin band and tucker of fine blond round the bust. The sleeve is short and full, the fulness tastefully arranged in festoons by four satin buttons, equidistant from each other: a little above the satin band that goes round the arm, on the shoulder, is a full-blown satin rose, with palmated satin leaves pending half way down the sleeve: broad satin band round the waist, with a rose and palmated leaves pendant behind. The skirt has an elegant satin border of roses surmounted with leaves, arranged in the form of the lotus, and united by festoons; beneath is a broad satin rouleau. White *crépe lisse* dress hat; the brim very full and rather broad, a little turned upwards all round, and ornamented with a garland of damask roses and two long white ostrich feathers, placed on the right side. Richly embroidered scolloped scarf of Urling's lace. Necklace and ear-rings of turquoise. Long white gloves; white satin shoes.

Promenade Dress
June 1824

PROMENADE DRESS

Pelisse of lilac *gros de Naples*, made quite plain, fastened down the front, and edged with a narrow cording of satin of the same colour: high standing collar, rounded at the corners, and projecting outwards. The sleeve large at the shoulder, and tapering gradually to the wrist, where it is finished with a sexangular cuff and buttons, and a worked muslin ruffle. The trimming is of the same material as the pelisse, and is formed into sextants by flat bands, with satin corded edges arranged perpendicularly; it approximates at the waist, widens as it reaches the shoulder, and also as it descends, till it unites with the trimming that goes round the bottom of the pelisse, which is finished with a double rouleau of satin. Rose-colour bonnet of *gros de Naples*, trimmed with the same, and edged with folded *crépe lisse*: bouquets of flowers are placed round the crown between the silk trimmings; the bonnet bent in front *à la Marie Stuart*, and tied under the chin with rose-colour *crépe lisse*. Cottage cap of British Mechlin lace, with bows of rose-colour crépe lisse on each side. Primrose-colour gloves; lilac kid shoes; green parasol, lined with lilac.

Ball Dress
June 1824

BALL DRESS

Dress of jonquil-colour silk *barége*, fancifully ornamented with satin bows of the same colour: the *corsage* made rather high: the stomacher of jonquil-colour satin, corded all round, and laced in front; it extends across the top of the bust, and ends nearly in a point at the waist, having bows arranged all round at equal distances: on the shoulder is a double row of satin puffing corded at the edges; satin *ceinture*, with triangular leaves formed into a rosette behind. The sleeve is very short, and decorated with satin bows, besides a net-work of satin with ornamented knots at each corner; it spreads over the top of the sleeve, and tapers almost to a point, where it unites with the double satin band that goes round the arm. The skirt has two rows of silk *barége* about half a quarter deep set on very full, and alternately ornamented with satin bows and a broad satin rouleau beneath. Turban of white *crépe lisse*, surmounting a broad band of gold net, richly ornamented with stars at each point, and two gold tassels pendant on the left side. Brilliant necklace of sapphire and diamonds; bracelets and ear-rings to correspond. White kid gloves; white satin shoes. French silk scarf of cerulean blue, with embroidered lace ends.

Promenade Dress
July 1824

PROMENADE DRESS

Pelisse of lavender-colour *gros de Naples*: the *corsage* made plain and close, displaying the beauty of the form; broad band of the same, edged with a double cording of satin, round the waist, which is rather long: the sleeves fuller than have been lately worn, and from the wrist nearly to the elbow, are three full puffings, confined with bands, and fastened by circular silk buttons: the epaulette is plain, being merely divided up the centre, and edged with a double cording of satin, which surrounds the whole of the pelisse and the trimmings: the bottom of the skirt has two broad rouleaus beneath a row of deep points, each finished with a silk button at top; the front ornamented to correspond. The trimming being placed longitudinally, and the points united by the buttons, as usual, the trimming is very broad at the bottom, lessens as it approaches the waist, and widens as it extends to the shoulders. Bonnet, manufactured from British grass, being a close imitation of the finest Leghorn; the brim broad, and standing out, except in the front, where it bends downwards: the crown is rather low, and has two large bows of lavender-colour gauze ribbon and two of yellow in front, with an intermixture of flowers. Cottage cap of net, with very full single border of Buckinghamshire lace, and a bunch of roses on the right side. The hair slightly parted on the forehead, and disposed in light curls. Gold chain and eye - glass. Primrose - colour gloves and shoes.

Opera Dress
July 1824

OPERA DRESS

Pink silk striped gossamer or gauze dress, the stripes having a narrow satin edge: the *corsage à la blouse*, and confined at the top with a narrow pink satin rouleau, ornamented with detached pink satin triangular corded leaves: the sleeves are very short and full, confined and regulated midway by pink satin leaves, which form a kind of wreath round the arm, being so arranged as to correspond with those on the bust: pink satin corded *ceinture*, fastened behind with hooks and eyes, beneath a rosette of triangular leaves. The skirt has a very full trimming of white tulle, tastefully decorated with pink satin diamonds, edged with tulle and satin, and drawn into a little fulness from the two opposite corners, and are placed up and down alternately, so as to form two rows. Opera hat of pink tulle and satin; the brim round, and deeper in the front and sides than behind: white marabouts, placed in front, fall over the crown, which is rather high. Necklace and ear-rings of pink topaz. White kid gloves; white satin shoes. Cachemire shawl.

Morning Dress
August 1824

MORNING DRESS

Dress of plain jaconot muslin; made high, and finished with a trimming of work round the throat: the front of the *corsage* and half way down the back is of fine book muslin, covered with corded waved bands of jaconot, trimmed with very narrow work, confined down the centre and at each end with buttons: long sleeve, plain at the back, and ornamented in front with corded trimmed bands, and fastened to the shoulder by buttons: small cuff edged with work, and confined at the wrist by a band and button. The skirt is made full, and long enough to touch the ground; and the trimming at the bottom of it is composed of graduated divisions of corded bands, trimmed with narrow work, and arranged in the form of fern-leaves or branches, with buttons down the centre, and a broad hem beneath. Cap (*à la baigneuse*) of white *crêpe lisse*; the border edged with rose-colour satin: the cap is in one piece, and the crown formed by a drawing of pink satin ribbon, which ties behind; lappets hang free from each side, or are fastened under the chin by being drawn through a fancy ring: a bouquet of flowers in front of the cap. *Ceinture* of shaded ribbon, with a gold buckle in front. Yellow kid shoes. Topaz ear-rings.

Ball Dress
August 1824

BALL DRESS

Dress of shaded blue silk *barège*; the *corsage* circular and moderately high: narrow tucker of fine blond; the stomacher composed of blue and white satin rouleaus, ornamented from the waist over the shoulder with sweet-briar roses: melon sleeve, terminated with sweet-briar roses at the band: a very deep full trimming of tulle round the bottom of the skirt, with a very broad blue satin rouleau at the top and bottom, and a wreath of full-blown roses in the middle. The hair dressed in large curls round the head, with a rose between each curl, forming a kind of regular garland. Necklace, ear-rings, and bracelets, of cornelian. White kid gloves. White satin shoes, and amber-colour silk scarf.

Morning Dress
September 1824

MORNING DRESS

Shaded yellow jaconot muslin dress; the stripes in waves, with small sprigs of gold colour: the *corsage en blouse*, and the long sleeves *en bouffants*, having seven divisions formed by corded bands, equidistant. Plain cuff, the size of the hand, with a neat worked muslin ruffle: corded band round the waist, with a plain gold buckle in front. The skirt is neatly trimmed with five double tucks, cut bias, and corded at the top and bottom: worked muslin square collar, fastened in front with a small gold buckle. Round cap of white *crèpe lisse*, drawn with amber-colour ribbon, and a large square lace veil. Wrought gold drop earrings. Yellow kid gloves and shoes.

Evening Dress
September 1824

EVENING DRESS

Dress of white *crèpe lisse*, ornamented with small sprigs of rose-colour floss silk: the *corsage* rather high, falls on each side of the bust, and is confined by a narrow pink satin band at the top, supporting a row of semicircles, which unite and point downwards: narrow tucker of fine blond. The sleeve is very short and full, and is decorated with four fancy bows, formed of four corded Persian lilac leaves, united by a knot: the sleeve is finished with a satin band, composed of three small rouleaus, and a vandyke blond lace beneath. The skirt has a deep *bouillonnée* of white tulle, cut bias, and headed with a band of three small rouleaus of pink satin: the same is introduced to confine the *bouillonnée* midway, and a broad rouleau is added beneath the small ones at the bottom, and two rows of pink satin bows, to correspond with the sleeves, are placed at regular distances in the *bouillonnée*. Large French bonnet of pink *crèpe lisse*, bent in front; the brim formed of double folds, and edged with pink satin and a narrow rouleau: the crown circular, with a trimming cut into eight oblong divisions, each bound with satin, and edged with folded *crèpe lisse:* four large white ostrich feathers are placed in the front. The hair dressed in light curls, and two full-blown white China roses on each side of the head. Emerald necklace, ear-rings, and bracelets. Long white kid gloves, white satin shoes, lace fichu, or silk élégantine.

94

Promenade Dress
October 1824

PROMENADE DRESS

Pelisse of lilac *gros de Naples*, made high and full, with a circular collar, which turns over, having a double cording at the edge. The sleeve is plain, and very large at the top, and confined twice between the shoulder and the elbow by corded satin bands, which are decorated about two or three inches apart on each side of the front of the sleeve by campanulas or Canterbury bells made of lilac satin. The skirt touches the ground, and is trimmed with five satin tucks of the same colour, elevated on the right side, and fastened by Canterbury bells of lilac satin: shaded lilac waist ribbon, and gold buckle in front. Very full worked muslin ruff, a little open at the throat, and fastened with a gold buckle. White chip bonnet, with a band of lilac satin introduced midway of the brim, which is circular, and deep in front, but shallow behind. The crown is low, and surrounded with a puffing of lilac satin ribbon and ears of corn: the strings are of *crèpe lisse* bound with lilac satin. Ear-rings of amethyst set in gold. Primrose-colour kid gloves and shoes.

Dinner Dress
October 1824

DINNER DRESS

Dress of black silk barège: the corsage made rather low and circular, and narrow on the shoulder: it is ornamented with satin hands placed longitudinally. The sleeve is very short and full, set in a hand of six small cords, and arranged in festoons, and fastened by buttons. The *ceinture* is of black satin corded with palmated leaves pendent behind, with buttons in the centre. The skirt has two very rich borders composed of satin rouleaus, formed into crescents, and united by two leaves of the Alpine saxifrage, tied at the base by a circlet composed of French folds; beneath are two satin rouleaus and a broad wadded hem. A large long sleeve of crape is added, and comes over the short one; it is something similar to the French manche a la neige, though without the redundant garniture. Turban of white crape, folded very small, and formed into large *bouffants*; broad and plain in front: the left side arranged in a full rosette, with alternate *bouffants* of white satin and crape; the right intermingling with the folds behind. Black necklace and ear-rings. White kid gloves and shoes.

Morning Dress
November 1824

MORNING DRESS

Dress of fawn-colour Thibet cloth, or English twilled cachemire; a warm and beautiful article for winter wear, falling into graceful folds, and unaffectedly displaying the elegance of form: the *corsage*, epaulette, and sleeve, are all *à la blouse*; the cuff finished with three bands, and worked muslin ruffles. The skirt has five cross or bias tucks, the same width as the ceinture, which fastens behind with a plain gold buckle; *collarette* of richly worked deep vandykes, tied in front with a cord and tassels. The hair *en grandes boucles*. French bonnet of *gros de Naples*, of the same colour as the dress; circular broad front, with a small rouleau of shaded terryvelvet, or *velours épingle* let in near the edge of the brim and round the crown, which is high and circular, and trimmed with shaded ribbon to correspond, arranged in puffs behind: in the front is a fanlike trimming of *gros de Naples*, cut bias, with shaded terry velvet near the edge; the choicest flowers of the winter season are disposed between, as the scarlet fuchsia, the sweet-scented everlasting, and the China rose. Plain gold ear-drops. Embroidered blue silk shawl, and fawn-colour morocco shoes.

Evening Dress
November 1824

EVENING DRESS

Dress of white worked barège: the corsage cut bias, and ornamented at the top, which is circular, by a folding of tulle, with a gold embroidered trimming à l' antique, and a narrow tucker of fine blond: the front is also embroidered with gold, in the form of a stomacher; and a gold embroidered band round the waist corresponds with the bands that confine the long full sleeves, which are arranged in seven *bouffants*, and are fastened at the wrist with topaz clasps. The skirt has an elegant trimming composed of three tucks of *barège*, with bands of tulle cut bias, and embroidered in gold *à l' antique;* beneath is a *bouillonńe* of *barège*, finished with a white satin rouleau. The hair is dressed in large and separate curls, or *boucles à la Francaise*; and on the right side is placed a cluster of rose-coloured passion-flowers, where a superb plume of white ostrich feathers is attached, and falls over to the left. Necklace and ear-rings of turquoise. White kid gloves and white satin shoes.

Morning Dress
December 1824

MORNING DRESS

Demi - blouse dress of rainbow-shaded *gros de Naples*; the waist long, and the *corsage* full and straight, and the stripes placed perpendicularly. The sleeves are of the *gigot de mouton* shape; the upper part being very large, and small towards the wrist, where a fulness is introduced and arranged by three flat bands, neatly corded with satin edges: at the bottom of the skirt are four wadded rouleaus of the same material as the dress, headed with narrow satin rouleaus and a broad wadded hem beneath. Lace or worked muslin frills, pelerines, or *collerettes*, are usually worn with high silk dresses: this in the print is a richly worked vandyke muslin pelerine, formed of two rows with long embroidered ends crossing over the bust, and confined by the *ceinture*, which is of *gros de Naples* edged with corded satin. The hair is dressed in large curls. Pale yellow gloves and shoes. Reticule of *ponceau* velvet, with gold chain, clasp, and ornaments.

Child s Dress: A short German frock-coat of superfine bottle-green cloth, with three rows of gilt buttons in front, and braided round the bottom of the skirt with a little tasteful ornament on each side. Nankeen vest, and trowsers trimmed at the ancles: worked Spanish collar, or fluted cambric frill.

Evening Dress
December 1824

EVENING DRESS

Gold-colour striped gossamer dress: the *corsage* cut straight, and rather high; the upper part full, and ornamented with narrow gold-colour satin rouleaus: a trimming of *bouffants*, separated by turban folds, rises from the waist and forms a stomacher front; it extends over the shoulder, and meets behind. The sleeve is short and full, and has a row of satin leaves emanating from the band, and spreading half way: the point of each leaf is fastened to a small corded satin band, and attached to the shoulder. Two rows of very full *bouffants*, fastened to the dress by gold-colour satin turban folds, ornament the bottom of the skirt. Dress hat of *crépe lisse*; the brim circular, with one puffing above and another beneath the edge. Round crown, ornamented with shaded satin ribbon and ostrich feathers of white and amber colour. Necklace, earrings, and bracelets of topaz and turquoise: the ear-rings large, and of the Chinese bell-shape. French trimmed white kid gloves and white satin shoes.

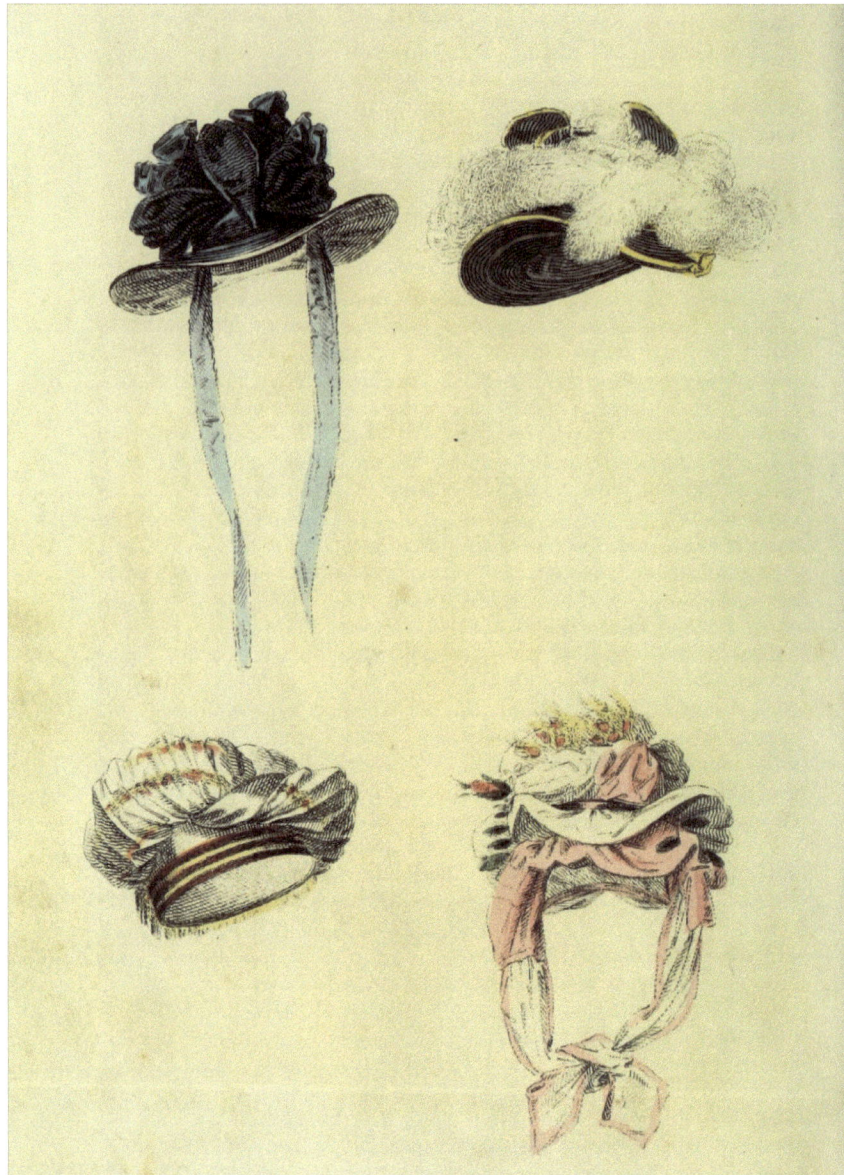

Head-Dresses
January 1825

HEAD-DRESSES

1. Bonnet of royal purple terry velvet or *velours épingle*; the brim broad and flat, with a corded satin edge; the crown high and rounded at the top, and partially covered with a *fichu* of velvet, bound with satin nearly half an inch in breadth, and ornamented with a small twisted silk cord of the same colour: the trimmings in front are large, and finished in the same manner; the centre one is long and narrow, and placed perpendicularly, concealing the termination of those on each side: bows of pearl-edge satin ribbon are disposed about the crown; long strings of the same inside the brim.

2. Black velvet dress hat, bound with gold lace; from a small bow in front, the brim forms double, and small white marabouts are introduced between; it is closed behind in a similar manner: broad gold band round the crown, and at the top four curved ornaments, bound also with gold lace; marabouts in front and on the right side.

3. Tartarian turban, formed of a richly shaded stripe silk kerchief.

4. Cap of pink and white *crèpe lisse*, with double border and broad strings of the same: the crown is high; the back part of white *crèpe lisse*, full, and arranged by five flat pink satin bands placed perpendicularly, and inserted in the pink satin band at the bottom of the caul: the front is formed by *bouffant* of alternate pink and white *crèpe lisse*, interspersed with pink satin ornaments of a papilionaceous shape, with a profusion of winter cherries or *alkekengi*, and rosebuds above.

Evening Dress
January 1825

EVENING DRESS

 Plain colour velvet dress: the *corsage* plain across the bust, and drawn to the shape with a little fulness at the waist; high in front, and falling rather lower on the shoulders, and finished with gold embroidered lace round the top: the sleeves are short, with epaulettes formed of heart-shaped leaves, trimmed with blond; attached are long full sleeves of white gauze, regulated in front by ribbon velvet passing from under the arm to the lower part of the sleeve, which is confined by three velvet bands round the arm, each fastened by a bow and gold clasp: blond ruffle at the wrist. At the bottom of the skirt is a broad band of satin of the same colour, with small silk cord laid across, forming squares: gold embroidered *ceinture*, in front with an antique gem. African turban of lilac *barège*, richly embroidered in gold, with a band of gold round the head, and supporting the folds over the right ear. The hair parted from the forehead, and three or four large curls on each side. Necklace of medallions in enamel, united by triple chains of gold ear-rings, to correspond. English Thibet square shawl with embroidered corners. Short white kid gloves; white satin shoes.

Promenade Dress
February 1825

PROMENADE DRESS

Wadded pelisse of *gros de Naples* of a bright geranium colour, lined with white sarsnet: the *corsage* made to the shape, with a square standing collar, edged with satin, and fastened in front with two gold buttons: broad *ceinture*, with satin corded edges, fastened in the same manner. Long full sleeve, confined between the shoulder and the elbow with a band and button, and five bands equidistant from the wrist towards the elbow. The front of the pelisse is ornamented with three bias tucks on each side, which meet at the waist, and increase in breadth and distance as they reach the shoulder, or descend to the bottom of the skirt, where they turn off circularly, and are continued round to the opposite side, where they unite with the tucks in front, and interlacing with them, form a festoon on each side; beneath is a broad wadded hem. Pamela hat of royal purple velvet; brim broad and circular, edged with a small rouleau of satin of the same colour as is the crown, which is rather high and large at the top: the hat is lined with satin, and trimmed with shaded gold-colour ribbon round the crown, and five bows and long ends, fringed on the right side; broad strings of the same withinside. Cottage cap of sprigged net, and full narrow border of British lace. Narrow frill and ruffles of the same. Long drop gold ear-rings and embossed gold chain twice round the throat. Dark sable muff. Yellow kid gloves and shoes.

Evening Dress
February 1825

EVENING DRESS

Ethereal blue satin striped gauze dress: the *corsage* plain in front, with a stomacher formed of blue satin laced with cord, and finished on each side with square satin tabs or straps *à l'Espagnol*; satin rouleau round the top, and narrow blond tucker. The sleeve short and full, and a double row of tabs, forming a wreath, is placed just above the band, which is edged with blond. A satin cape with square corners (divided on the shoulder) extends from the stomacher round the back of the *corsage*, and is also trimmed with narrow blond. Sash of blue satin, fastened at the side with a gold buckle. The bottom of the dress is decorated with a row or wreath of lunulated or crescent-shaped leaves edged with blond, and ornamented in the centre I with a sort of chain composed of French folds of satin; two narrow rouleaus of satin and a broad wadded hem beneath. The hair is arranged in large curls in front and at the top of the head, and a blue gauze scarf is tastefully disposed between; on the left side are two bows and ends fringed with gold. Gold necklace, with a brilliant ornament in form of a star in front; ear-rings to correspond. Long white kid gloves; white satin shoes; crimson-shaded silk kerchief.

Promenade Dress
March 1825

PROMENADE DRESS

Coral-colour *gros de Naples* high dress: the *corsage* made to the shape in front, with a little fulness at the bottom of the waist behind: the sleeve *en gigot*, that is, very large at the top, and confined towards the wrist with five corded bands, each about half an inch in breadth; as the sleeves finish at the wrist, cuffs are requisite, which are usually of embroidered French cambric, of the same pattern as the *collerette*. The front of the *corsage* has a fancy bow in the centre, and three more are placed at equal distances down the front of the skirt: on each side are two bias tucks of the same material as the dress, edged on one side with a narrow, satin cord; they approximate at the waist, extend to the shoulder and towards the feet, where they turn off circularly to trim the bottom of the dress; wadded hem beneath. Hat of coral *gros de Naples;* brim broad and circular in front, but much shallower behind; the crown large and projecting forward, composed of six divisions, the points meeting in the centre at the top; a bouquet of fancy flowers on the right side: strings inside the brim. Hyacinthine or deep blue silk mantle, lined with ermine, and trimmed round the bottom with a deep border of the same. Shoes of blue Morocco. Light yellow kid gloves.

105

Ball Dress
March 1825

BALL DRESS

Dress of pale pink gauze, or *crèpe lisse*, over a white satin slip: the *corsage à la saubrette*, being made to the shape, and laced with pink cord both in the front and back, with an angular drapery edged with white satin; the points brought to the centre, and extending half way down the *corsage*, which is straight across the bust, and very low on the shoulders: the waist is finished with straps, that in the centre being the widest, and bound with pink satin. The sleeve is extremely short and full, and supported with six shaded pink satin rouleaus, formed into a loop and ring, the latter half concealed in the *bouillonnèe* of the sleeve. The bottom of the dress is trimmed to correspond, having a very full and deep *bouillonnèe*, surmounted by full-blown pale China roses united by green leaves; from each rose a shaded pink satin rouleau extends over the *bouillonnèe* and is fastened through the rings, which are arranged at regular distances, and rest on the wadded hem beneath. The hair is parted on the forehead, and in large curls, intermixed with bows or *noeuds* of pink and hair-colour *crèpe lisse*; with primroses and poppy-anemones. A very elegant necklace of emeralds, with a brilliant star, or *croix de St. Louis*, in front; ear-rings and bracelets to correspond. Long white kid gloves; white satin shoes; circular ivory fan.

Morning Dress
April 1825

MORNING DRESS

Pelisse of Pomona or apple-green *gros de Naples*, fastened in front with circular silk buttons of the same colour; a single rouleau, about an inch and a half broad, surrounds the edge of the skirt just above the wadded hem. The *corsage* fits the shape, and the sleeve is *en gigot*, but not to that extreme size which has been; it is slit at the wrist, and buttons, and has a neat row of small oblong ornaments near the edge: the band of the waist is corded, and buttons. The pelerine or cape is composed of alternate rows of *gros de naples* or ribbon, the colour of the pelisse, and of myrtle green: it is notched or vandyked the breadth of each division. Square embroidered *collerette* of French cambric. Hat formed, like the pelerine, of two shades of green; the brim broad, flat, and circular in front; the crown plain at the top, and rather full all round; a bouquet of hyacinth or haw-bells and blossoms of the mezerion on the left side. Gold ear-rings, and bracelets outside the sleeves; chain and eye-glass. Pale yellow gloves; bronze-colour parasol and shoes.

Dinner Dress
April 1825

DINNER DRESS

Cerulean blue *crèpe lisse* dress worn over a white satin slip; the *corsage* rather high over the bust, and plain, but drawn behind; narrow satin band round the top. The sleeve short and full, and regulated by small satin stars. A diamond satin, trimming, ornamented with a chain of *crèpe lisse* puffs or *bouffants*, crosses the bust in form of a stomacher, and from the waist downwards gradually extends in width till it turns off circularly, to form a border just above a narrow satin rouleau that heads a broad wadded hem at the bottom of the skirt. The hair is *en grandes boucles*, with bands of pearl and bows, or *mends* of blue satin, intermixed. Gold necklace and large medallion in front; armlet and bracelet of gold, fastened by medallion clasps. Long white kid gloves, white satin shoes, carved cedar fan.

Morning Dress
May 1825

MORNING DRESS

Dress of lilac *gros tie Naples*: the *corsage* plain, rather high in front, broad on the shoulders, and edged with a double satin rouleau of the same colour; it fastens behind with hooks and eyes. The upper part of the sleeve is full; below the elbow it has three satin bands equidistant, and tied in bows on the outside of the arm: the wrist is finished with a double satin rouleau and embroidered cambric ruffles. The skirt is very neatly ornamented with waving satin bands, a quarter of a yard deep, fastened at the top with silk buttons, and inserted within the broad satin rouleau at the edge of the dress: corded *ceinture*, ornamented in front with six silk buttons. Lace *fichu*, scolloped at the edge and richly embroidered; it crosses in front, and ties in a small bow behind. The hair is parted, and arranged in large regular curls on each side. Gold ear-rings, bracelets, chain, and eyeglass. The necklace is formed of a black ribbon, with a small elegant embossed gold rosette at the throat, from which the ribbon descends, and a large richly ornamented gold cross is suspended, nearly reaching to the *ceinture*. Morocco shoes.

Evening Dress
May 1825

EVENING DRESS

Elegant dress of Urling's lace, with Brussels sprigs: the *corsage* full, circular round the bust, and trimmed with a falling lace: the sleeves short and regularly full. The fulness of the skirt is not entirely set in the band at the back, but slightly introduced in the front and sides, which has a very pleasing effect with dresses of so light and delicate a texture. Half way of the skirt is a very elegant row of flowers in separate clusters, and beneath are two deep flounces of rich lace, separated by a simple wreath of leaves: the edge of the skirt is scolloped, and a richly embroidered dwarf cistus fills up each space. Blue satin sash, with an embossed gold buckle on the right side. Blue satin slip. Turban of blue satin; the band composed of four longitudinal folds, and a row of French pearls at the edge; the satin full and double round the crown, and two long white ostrich feathers falling backwards. Necklace of pearl, fastened in front with an elegant gold clasp, ornamented with rubies and pearls. Ear-rings and bracelets to correspond. White kid gloves; white satin shoes.

Dinner Dress
June 1825

DINNER DRESS

Canary-Yellow *gros de Naples*; the *corsage* bias, plain, and made to fit the shape: it is trimmed at the top of the bust with two rows of ribbon of the same colour, put on very full, and fluted; it is very prettily rounded in front, and retires a little off the shoulder. Short sleeve, moderately full, beneath a white *crèpe lisse* full long sleeve, confined at the wrist with a broad gold bracelet, with embossed gold snaps, and a row of turquois above. The dress is decorated with ornamented silk cords, which approximate at the waist, and extend as they ascend the *corsage*, or descend the skirt: each cord is inserted into a double circlet, which unites the points of a row of deep festoons, formed of fluted ribbon, corresponding with the trimming of the bust: a broad rouleau surrounds the edge of the dress, which just touches the ground: broad satin sash of canary-yellow. Silk dress hat, with a gold ornament in front, and a full plume of white ostrich feathers; one is placed beneath the brim, and falls low on the right side of the face. Necklace and ear-rings of different coloured gems set in gold; gold chain and eye - glass. White kid gloves; white satin shoes.

111

Ball Dress
June 1825

BALL DRESS

Dress of white crape; the *corsage* ornamented in front with a full-blown satin rose, with rose-colour tulip-leaves emanating from it and extending over the bust, their points reaching to the *ceinture*. Short sleeve, set in a white satin band round the arm, and moderately full; in the centre is a rose, with a pink satin lotus, edged with white satin, rising above it. The skirt is terminated by a broad rose-colour satin rouleau, above which are bouquets of flowers, each surmounted by a rose-colour lotus, edged with white satin. Sash of rose colour, with long ends fringed, and fastened with a brilliant buckle on the right side. The hair is in large curls, with satin leaves in front, and an ornamented gold pin placed transversely towards the left side. Rich embroidered blond scarf. Delicately wrought gold necklace and ear-rings. Long white kid gloves; white satin shoes. Transparent painted fan.

Promenade Dress
July 1825

PROMENADE DRESS

Pelisse of lilac *gros de Naples*; the collar stiffened, and turned half over; the *corsage* is made full longitudinally, and confined by a band and a row of lilac silk buttons down the centre of the front and back; the shoulders also have a band, but without buttons. The sleeves are *en gigot*, neatly finished with bands at the wrist: the *ceinture* is rather broad, and ornamented behind by two silk frogs of the same colour as the pelisse; a rouleau of the same breadth as the hem, and separated by a space of equal width, surrounds the bottom of the skirt, which is long and full. *Cornette* of tulle, with a narrow full border. Bonnet of British Leghorn, very fine and light; the brim broad and open; the crown rather low, and trimmed with double white *crêpe lisse* edged with blue satin, beginning at the bottom of the crown in front, and rising across to the top at the back, where it is formed into a tasteful bow. Brussels lace veil. Straw-colour shoes and gloves; green parasol, lined with pale rose-colour sarsnet.

Evening Dress
July 1825

EVENING DRESS

Dress of jonquil-colour *crèpe lisse* over a white satin slip; the *corsage* made plain, but ornamented in the front and at the back with six perpendicular satin rouleaus, rather approximating at the waist, and terminating beneath a white satin band across the top of the bust: small satin orange-leaves are placed directly over each rouleau. The sleeves are short and full, and have a trimming of folded *crèpe lisse* round the arm, and up the centre a wreath of orange-leaves in satin. The skirt is ornamented about a third of its depth, with three satin tucks between each; large orange-leaves in satin are placed near, but not to touch: broad satin sash, with long ends fringed, fastened on the left side by a brilliant amethyst buckle. The hair in large curls, with bows of shaded jonquil-colour gauze ribbon interspersed. Necklace of graduated amethysts; ear-rings and bracelets to suit. Stripe gauze *fichu*, or handkerchief of white and amethyst colour. Long white kid gloves, and white satin shoes.

Morning Dress
August 1825

MORNING DRESS

Dress of plain jaconot muslin; the *corsage* full at the back, and ornamented in front with insertion-work, which proceeds outwardly from the shoulder to nearly the centre of the waist, inclosing four rows of very delicate work, placed transversely between the muslin, and meeting in points in the front. The sleeves long and full, with three rows of insertion-work near the wrist. The skirt has three broad rows of insertion-lace-work, of an elegant and novel pattern. *Ceinture* of garter-blue ribbon, with a silver buckle in front. White *crèpe lisse* cap, of a circular or dome shape; the crown irradiating from the top in large flutes, which are edged with small blue satin piping, and contain each a half-blown rose, or a rose-colour gauze bow; beneath is a drawn head-piece and border of folded *crèpe lisse*, interspersed with blue and rose-colour gauze ribbon corresponding to the bow at the top: lappet strings of the same material as the cap. Broad gold bracelets and plain gold earrings. Silk *barège* shawl; yellow gloves and shoes.

Dinner Dress
August 1825

DINNER DRESS

Dress of pink *gros de Naples*; the *corsage* made low, and slashed perpendicularly, to admit of white *gros de Naples* puffings. Long sleeve, moderately large, except the top, which is of white *gros de Naples*, exceedingly full, and confined by five bands of pink *gros de Naples*, and finished with a row of pearl drops or *campanettes*; the remainder of the sleeve has five rows of white *gros de Naples* let in downwards, and four bracelet bands equidistant; that at the wrist confining the glove, the sleeve not extending over the hand. The front of the dress is ornamented by oval puffs of white *gros de Naples*, gradually increasing in size as they descend; a *campanette* or small pearl bell is attached to the outside of each; and on each side of this trimming is a satin cord supporting pink oval puffs, with pearl bells pendant by the cord, and pearl beads fastening the other end: this trimming flows off circularly from the front, and is continued round the dress, above a wreath similarly formed, but with puffs on each side the cord, with alternate leaves of white *gros de Naples*; wadded hem beneath white *crèpe lisse* tucker, confined in folds by several gold sliders. The hair, as usual, arranged in large curls, but tastefully disposed among bows of blue satin. Necklace and ear-rings of pearl, turquoise, and gold. White kid gloves and white satin shoes.

Morning Dress
September 1825

MORNING DRESS

Dress of fine jaconot muslin, ornamented with rose-colour satin ribbon and clear book muslin; the *corsage* full and rather high, with three small rows of puffed book muslin round the top, rose-colour satin being drawn through the centre row, and tied behind: on each side of the bust, and nearly meeting at the waist, is a very full piece of book muslin, drawn at four equal distances with rose-colour satin, of which a loop or bell is formed on the outside of each drawing. Long sleeve, of an easy fulness, with three drawings towards the wrist; at the shoulder four deep vandykes of book muslin made very full, and drawn with rose-colour satin on the outside, each point fastened to the sleeve by a rose-colour bow. The border of the skirt, about a quarter of a yard in depth, is prettily composed of very full book muslin, with perpendicular drawings of rose-colour satin, terminating with a bow at the top; every other drawing being but half the height of the intervening one, has a very pleasing effect. Cape or pelerine of the same material as the dress, rounded off from the front, where it is fastened with an oval amethyst brooch, and trimmed round with two rouleaus of puffed book muslin, rose-colour satin being drawn through one. Chip hat, trimmed with flowers; and rose-colour *crèpe lisse* gauze veil. Lemon - colour gloves, and morocco shoes.

CHILD S DRESS

Dark green Highland plaid dress; rose-colour tartan stockings; Highland cap and feathers.

117

Evening Dress
September 1825

EVENING DRESS

Azure *crèpe lisse* dress, over a white satin slip; the *corsage* rather long and full, and arranged in small regular perpendicular plaits, of a moderate height, and finished at the top with a pale azure satin band. The sleeve short and full, with three satin bands extending downwards from the shoulder; at each end is a satin marguerite, and in the centre an ornament composed of six satin leaves, three on each side of the band which conceals their base. The skirt has two rows of a similar trimming, only larger, and the marguerite is placed on the band filling the space which the curve lines of the leaves form; beneath is a broad rouleau. Azure satin sash. Hat a *demi-pelerine* of white *crèpe lisse*, crossed with silk cord, and a button at each point; the brim edged with white satin and fine narrow blond lace: the crown is *en marmotte*, each recess edged with satin, and a full-blown Provence rose within; a bouquet of rose-buds on each side of the crown. The hair in large curls. Ear-rings of turquoise; broad necklace and bracelets of small pearl, and gold beads with ornaments of rubies. Gold watch and chain, with various fancy trinkets. Long white kid gloves. White satin shoes. Rainbow shaded gauze fan.

Head-Dresses
October 1825

HEAD-DRESSES

1. Fine British Leghorn hat; the brim large, flat, and of equal breadth; the crown moderately high; round it is a lilac satin ribbon, with a bow on the left side, from which rises a fanciful trimming in lilac *gros de Naples*, edged with straw-colour satin, terminating at the top of the crown a little beyond the front. Another trimming is introduced midway, and rising circularly, finishes with a small bouquet of fancy flowers on the left side: a bouquet is also placed on the right side, but higher. Strings of lilac satin, and a bow on the right, inside the brim.

2. Turban of scarlet or pomegranate-colour *crèpe lisse*, with large close longitudinal folds, confined in front by a broad gold band placed obliquely: the head-piece of *gros de Nap*les, pointed in front, and edged with gold lace.

3. Cap of white *crèpe lisse*; the crown circular, and formed by two rows of large puffs, edged with pink satin, having a wreath of China roses beneath the upper row, and round the head-piece, within each puff, a sprig of arbutus and geranium: the border is very full and deep, and ties under the chin with pink satin ribbon.

4. Pale blue gauze dress hat, fluted, and the brim edged with narrow blond; the crown surrounded by a wreath of blue satin leaves, tied in pairs by a satin knot, each leaf deeply notched. White ostrich feathers are tastefully arranged round the crown, the highest being in the front.

Evening Dress
October 1825

EVENING DRESS

Dress of pink *gros de Naples*; the *corsage* of a moderate height, with a slight fulness in front, and crossed with a thin drapery of folded gauze of the same colour, beginning at the shoulder, with a pink satin star composed of four leaves, each leaf having one deep notch, and a knot or button in the centre of the star uniting the points of the leaves. The sleeve is full and very short, and has five divisions, each formed by two satin notched leaves, united by a button, and placed perpendicularly round the sleeve. The skirt has a rich border of *crèpe lisse bouffant*, with pairs of notched leaves, arranged to correspond with the sleeves: abroad satin rouleau heads the trimming, and at the bottom is a wadded hem; above is a row of *crèpe lisse* puffs, placed obliquely, and fastened at the top with a small satin button, and finished at the opposite end with three pink satin notched leaves, united by a button. Broad satin sash, with a gold buckle on the left side, and two small bows; the ends long and fringed. White *crèpe lisse* tucker, and long full sleeves, confined by broad gold bracelets. The hair dressed in large curls. Gold ear-rings and gold chain and eye-glass. White satin shoes, and short white kid gloves.

Garden Costume
November 1825

GARDEN COSTUME

Pelisse of Pomona-green *gros de Naples*, open in front, and lined with pale pink sarsnet: plain collar, sloped off from the front, stiffened, and half turned, so as to display the pink lining and the neat embroidered frill round the throat: the *corsage* full, and of such a length as to shew an elegant shape to advantage: the sleeve large, and confined above the wrist by a band and small oval buckle, and, secondly, by a broad gold bracelet: straight cuff, slit as far as the wrist: corded band round the waist, fastened by a gold buckle on the right side. Plain jaconot muslin high dress: the *corsage* made to fit, and elegantly worked: the skirt scolloped at the edge, and ornamented with three deep tucks, and insertion-work between. Hair in graceful ringlets *à la Vandyke*, partly covered by a beautifully embroidered lace veil. Necklace of red cornelian, worn outside the pelisse; ear-rings to correspond. Lemon-colour gloves; purple morocco shoes; rose-colour parasol, lined with white, and an antique wreath round the edge.

121

Evening Dress
November 1825

EVENING DRESS

Silk *barèges* dress of citron-colour: the corsage arranged in small perpendicular plaits, rather high across the front of the bust, where it is straight, and set in a broad band, ornamented with a row of *rosa salvatira:* the shoulder-strap is broad and plain: the sleeve short, and composed of two rows of vandykes, the points meeting in the centre of the sleeve, and forming squares or diamonds between, which are of white satin, ornamented with a full-blown China rose in each; the sleeve is terminated with narrow vandyke blond lace, the same as the tucker. The skirt has a deep border, headed with a band of citron-colour *gros de Naples*, with pendant straps, supporting a drapery of the same material formed into vandykes, edged with satin, and uniting with a row beneath by a satin button, and displaying the white satin diamonds with roses in their centre, corresponding with the sleeve; wadded hem beneath, attached by straps to the vandykes above; fancy buckle of different-coloured gems, fastening a broad ribbon with three ends of various lengths under the left arm. Turban of citron-colour *crèpe lisse*, divided into *bouffants* by bands of the same colour in satin as is the head-piece, which has two rows of French beads round the edge. Necklace, three delicate chains of gold, fastened in front by a beautiful ornament of pearl and turquoise: ear-rings to suit: bracelets of broad gold, studded with rubies, outside the gloves, which are long, and of white kid. White satin shoes.

Morning Dress
December 1825

MORNING DRESS

Dress of lavender-colour *gros de Naples*: the *corsage* made rather high, and shaped at the back; the fulness regulated at the top by three narrow bands, or silk braid of the same colour: the sleeve full and long, confined at the wrist with three ornaments of different lengths, narrowing towards the cuff. The skirt is tastefully trimmed with four notched rows of the same material as the dress, two of the rows pointing upwards, the others falling downwards, and a fluted band, encircled with a rouleau, adorns the centre; beneath is a wadded hem. Epaulette braces, of pink and white *gros de Naples*, meet in a point behind, extend in a slanting direction to the shoulders, cross in front, with long ends loose from the *ceinture*, which is the same as the dress: the epaulette is trimmed with a double row of pink and white quilled ribbon. The cap is made to correspond, being formed of pink and white and lilac *gros de Naples*, and a border of Grecian lace; two rouleaus extend across the crown, composed of the three different colours; the hinder-most has a bow of pink ribbon attached, the same as the strings. Lilac kid shoes.

Evening Dress
December 1825

EVENING DRESS

Dress of pomegranate colour or scarlet *gros de Naples*: the *corsage* made to fit the shape, square across the bust, and rather high; the fulness longitudinal, and regulated by seven perpendicular bands, equidistant, slightly approximating at the waist; the back is full, with five bands to correspond, and fastened with hooks and eyes: the sleeve is short and full, with three divisions, one in the centre, front, and back, formed by a triple bow, or three emarginate leaves, united by a *bacca*, or berry; the sleeve is finished by a corded band. The skirt is ornamented with four rows of rouleaus, arranged in an antique pattern, each uniting with the one beneath, and forming a neat and novel border.

Head-dress composed of a broad band of scarlet and yellow *crèpe lisse* and French beads, with a large uniform bow on the right side, with two rows of beads across the centre. The hair divided in front, two large curls on the temples, and ringlets on each side; the hair very tastefully arranged at the top and back. Chain of gold round the neck, and a row of pearl. Long pearl ear-rings set in gold; broad bracelets of coloured beads outside the gloves, which are of white kid. White satin shoes.

124

Promenade Dress
January 1826

PROMENADE DRESS

Pelisse of *satin Turque*, or Turkish satin, of a rich myrtle-green, wadded, and lined with rose-coloured sarsnet: the *corsage* made the straight way, and full both in the back and front, and set in gathers in the band; it closes in front, and is ornamented from the throat to the feet with large mother-of-pearl buttons: the sleeves are of a moderate width, and terminated at the wrist with a plain double-corded band: double pelerine or cape deeply vandyked, and edged with very narrow chinchilli fur, to correspond with the muff and the broad chinchilli fur at the bottom of the skirt. Buttons and trimmings (when not of fur) are generally of the same material as the pelisse. Black velvet hat, of a moderate size, bent in front; the crown ornamented with a profusion of velvet bows, and a gold slider in the centre: rose-colour strings, the same as the ribbon round the throat, which ties in two bows and long ends, supporting the *collerette* of worked muslin. The hair in ringlets; and cap *à trois pièces*, with a narrow full border, fastened under the chin. High walking shoes of black leather, lined and edged with fur.

125

Evening Dress
January 1826

EVENING DRESS

Dress of geranium-colour *gros de Naples:* the *corsage* made to fit the shape; rather high in front, but lower on the shoulders, and trimmed round the top with a notched *ruche* of the same material; a light folded drapery, in the form of a stomacher, adorns the bust. The sleeve is short and extremely full, and set in a satin corded band, with long white *crèpe lisse* sleeves inserted at the shoulder, and confined at the wrist with broad bead bracelets and ornamented *mancherons*. The skirt is made to wrap, and flows off from the left side, and is shaped circularly on the right, just above the wadded hem of the petticoat (which is of the same *gros de Naples* as the dress), and is trimmed with two double *ruches*, deeply notched, which have a very pretty effect, particularly when made of the Italian patent crape (manufactured by Noailles*), the transparency and richness of which are universally allowed. Indeed this article bids fair to resume its station for full dress among the *haul ton*, as, from its superiority in texture and appearance, it must ever be a favourite with those *élégantes* who prefer excellence to cheapness. The *ceinture* is of *gros de Naples*, edged with corded satin of the same colour, and supporting a gold watch set with rubies, and gold chain and trinkets. The hair is in large curls, and forms a kind of antique wreath round the head; a cluster of winter-flowers is placed on the right side. Ear-rings of pearl and gold; shaded gauze scarf; white satin shoes.

We are indebted to Miss Davis of Charlotte-street for the evening dress and also for both of those of the last month.

* Manufactory at Greatness, Kent.

126

Dinner Dress
February 1826

DINNER DRESS

Turkish satin dress of lemon-colour, closed in front, and ornamented with buttons of the same material, placed very near each other; the *corsage* rather high, but declining from the shoulder; a rouleau "*en serpent,*" fastened by a circlet in the front just above the *ceinture*, rises to the shoulder, where another circlet confines it, and passing over, ornaments the back in a similar manner. The sleeve is short and full, with a band of the same width as that at the top of the *corsage*, and is prettily decorated with five trimmings formed of double plaits, regulated by a rouleau in the centre, extending the length of the sleeve. The skirt has a light and elegant border, composed of two rouleaus, placed in a waving direction; and from a circlet that encompasses the lower part of the wave, proceeds an ornament corresponding to those on the sleeve; the rouleau in the centre is terminated by a button, and arranged semicircularly, so as to fill the space formed by the rising of the rouleau; beneath is a broad wadded hem. The sash is long, and of the same colour as the dress, but richly adorned with shaded leaves of a deeper hue, and fastened on the right side with a highly wrought gold buckle. White satin hat, edged with chenille, turned up in front, and confined by a loop of citron-colour Italian crape, proceeding from the crown, and fastened by an elegant pearl ornament, with a large ruby in the centre; bird of Paradise on the right side, and bows of citron-colour Italian crape. The hair slightly parted and arranged in one row of neat curls, and a fullblown China rose on the right side. Pearl necklace, fastened by a ruby clasp; medallion bracelets, outside the long gloves; shoes of the same material as the dress.

Evening Dress
February 1826

EVENING DRESS

Pale scarlet Italian crape dress over a white satin slip; the *corsage* full, and confined with a band, high in front, but lower in the shoulders: it is ornamented in a new and elegant style. From the centre of the bust to the right shoulder are three rouleaus of shaded scarlet satin; they commence with a palmatum, or ornament of four shaded satin leaves pointing upwards, and the rouleaus extend across the bust in a waving direction to the left side, where they unite with six satin rouleaus, descending to the trimming of the skirt, which consists of a very deep and full drapery of crape; here they are nearly a quarter of a yard apart, and sustain the drapery in festoons, each division having three palmatum ornaments equidistant. The drapery in front reaches to the white satin rouleau of the slip, but rises considerably at the sides. This rouleau is ornamented with stripes, placed at regular distances, and attached by buttons on the upper side; beneath is a wadded hem. The short sleeve is full, and resting on the band; in the centre is a palmatum ornament. The long sleeve of white *crêpe lisse* is very full, but fitted to the wrist with three bands and broad bracelets of gold studded with amethysts. The *ceinture* is richly embroidered. The head-dress is composed of two rows of Italian crape *en bouffants*, with a bow and embroidered end on the right side, and supported in the centre with a band of plaited hair and a beautiful oval gem. Ear-rings and necklace of gold and amethysts; short white kid gloves; white satin shoes. The above are from the tasteful fancy of Miss Davis of Charlotte-street.

Dinner Dress
March 1826

DINNER DRESS

A bright fawn-colour dress of English *gros de Naples*, trimmed round the top of the bust with ribbon of the same colour *en tuyau*, with a second row on the shoulder. The sleeve is short and full, and furnished with a band and narrower trimming. The *corsage* is rather long, a little full, confined by a *ceinture*, which has a rosette and short ends behind of the same material as the dress. The skirt has an elegant yet simple border of the same colour, either of Italian crape or English *gros de Naples*, consisting of a rose *en tuyau*, with a satin piping passing along the centre, forming a double narrow flounce, one standing up, the other falling downwards; the same is repeated at the edge of the dress, and between is a trimming *à l'antique*, composed of satin scrolls, ornamented on the outside with separate bows placed close to each other.

The head-dress is of white Italian crape, entwined with gold lace, and red China roses interspersed tastefully; and the hair in large regular curls. Long white kid gloves; a broad gold bracelet on one arm, and on the other a fancy chain of gold and emeralds corresponding with the necklace, which has a beautiful emerald locket in the centre: drop-earrings to suit; jocko fan; white satin shoes.

Ball Dress
March 1826

BALL DRESS

Dress of fine tulle over a white satin slip; the *corsage* high across the bust, but lower in proportion in the shoulders, and bound with white satin, from which falls a deep blond scolloped lace, doubled on the shoulders, and forming a kind of epaulette to the short full sleeve, which fits tight round the arm, and is finished with a narrower scolloped blond lace. A Provins rose is placed on the left side of the bust, and a satin corkscrew trimming in the form of a stomacher regulates the fulness of the *corsage*, which is longitudinal. The skirt is ornamented with two rows of festoons, edged with three narrow pipings of cherry-coloured satin, the centre of the upper festoon being attached to the points of the lower by a full-blown Provins rose, suspended by a narrow white satin corkscrew trimming; in the lower festoon the roses are attached to the broad white satin rouleau at the bottom of the dress; a bouquet of Provins roses and Eastern hyacinths is placed at the termination of each festoon of the upper row. Broad satin sash of cherry-colour, tied (in two short bows and long ends fringed) on the left side. The hair is divided in the Madonna style, and ornamented with an elegant wreath of French pearl beads and full-blown Provins roses, brought from behind the right ear to the front, and entwining a bow of hair on the crown of the head. Elegant blond spotted scarf; long white kid gloves, with bracelets outside. Necklace and ear-rings of white cornelian and embossed gold; white satin shoes.

YOUNG LADY'S DRESS

Frock of white *crèpe lisse*; the *corsage* full and edged with ethereal blue satin, and a narrow trimming of blond lace beneath; the sleeves short and full. The skirt is ornamented with four pipings of blue satin; three rise circularly half way up the left side, and are terminated with blue satin bows. Blue satin slip, the length of the frock; white cambric trowsers, finished with delicately scolloped work, and ornamented with two pipings of blue satin; broad blue satin sash tied behind. The hair parted in front, and in ringlets *à la Vandyke*. Pearl necklace, gold chain, and cornelian heart; gold bracelets outside the long white kid gloves; white silk stockings; blue satin shoes, with sandals.

Carriage Costume
April 1826

CARRIAGE COSTUME

Pelisse of Turkish satin of a bright blue or hyacinthine colour, lined with white sarsnet and fastened in front; the collar square and turned down; the *corsage* plain and close to the shape, and ornamented on each side with a row of diamonds of the same material as the dress, edged with a narrow satin rouleau of the same colour, and united with a satin button. The two rows diverge towards the shoulders and meet in front at the waist, where the diamonds unite in pairs, and gradually increase in size as they descend; two rows of swansdown adorn the bottom of the dress, between which is an elegant satin scroll. The sleeve is still *en gigot*, but much smaller from the elbow to the wrist, which has three diamond ornaments to correspond, placed perpendicularly. The *ceinture* has a highly wrought gold buckle in front; deep square collerette of British Brussels lace; cap of white *crèpe lisse*; a bouquet of damask roses on the right side, and others variously disposed. The hair in large curls, arranged to accord with the border of the cap, which is full, and of folded *crèpe lisse*. Gold ear-rings and bracelets; gold chain and eye-glass; jonquil-colour kid gloves and shoes.

Evening Dress
April 1826

EVENING DRESS

Beautifully sprigged Urling's lace dress, over a primrose-colour Turkish satin slip, made with a frock-body of a moderate height and fulness, confined at the top with a narrow satin rouleau, and trimmed with a row of deep falling lace, put on very full. The sleeve is short and extremely full, and finished with the same kind of lace as that round the bust, and equally full. The skirt has an elegant wreath of various sorts of flowers, surmounting two very deep flounces of rich scollop lace, which are headed with satin piping, and put on with much taste, slightly partaking of the festoon; the rise of the upper flounce is opposite to where the lower recedes, and displays a well-arranged selection of flowers within each space; a wreath of single leaves and a row of rich scollops terminate the dress. The *ceinture* has a beautiful cameo in front. A rouleau of primrose and hair-colour *gros de Naples* forms the head-dress; and the hair is disposed in ringlets, a far more becoming and elegant style than the stiff large curls which have disguised the beautiful tresses of our fair fashionables. Shaded gauze scarf; pearl ear-rings and necklace, with a gold chain; broad cameo bracelets outside the gloves, which are long white kid and French trimmed; white satin shoes. We are indebted, to Miss Davis, of Charlotte-street, for the above elegant costumes.

Morning Dress
May 1826

MORNING DRESS

Dress of sea-green *gros de Naples*; the *corsage* made to fit the shape, rather high, and ornamented with nine corded bands, placed longitudinally and equidistant at the sides, but formed into three separate divisions in front, each uniting three bands and confined with a button. The sleeves are very large and full to the elbow, where they gradually decrease and become quite plain at the wrist, and are terminated in a corded band; the fulness is regulated by a broad band which extends from the shoulder downwards. The skirt is decorated with bows and festoons of ribbon of the same colour, supporting Italian crape baskets of a light and elegant form, the centre projecting, and the top and bottom terminating in points; the lowest ribbon is caught up by the one above between every basket, thus giving great variety to the festoons; broad wadded hem beneath: fluted muslin *collerette*, shallow in front, but widening as it proceeds towards the shoulder, and fastened by a cameo. Gold chain and eye-glass. The hair arranged in large curls, and a gold comb confining a long bow of hair on the top of the head; gold earrings and bracelets; shaded ribbon reticule, of a similar shape to the baskets that ornament the dress; yellow gloves and shoes.

Ball Dress
May 1826

BALL DRESS

Crèpe-lisse dress of Haytian blue; the *corsage* plain and close to the shape, with a narrow notched tucker and Farinet folds of white *crèpe lisse* across the bust, and a small bouquet of spring flowers in front. The sleeves rather low on the shoulder, short and full, and ornamented with two notched *ruches* of white *crèpe lisse*, and a narrow blue satin rouleau; the lower extending all round the arm, midway of the sleeve; the other only across the top. The skirt is ornamented with a row of Persian roses, attached by bows of blue satin ribbon, two of the ends extending to a handsome wreath of *folia peltata* in blue satin, the stalks of which are arranged circularly from the one to the other; a row of puffed *crèpe lisse*, and a narrow satin wadded hem, terminate the bottom of the dress. Blue satin sash, with short bows and long ends, fastened on the left side, leather below the band of the waist. Head-dress of three folds of Haytian blue *crèpe lisse*, with four rows of pearl beneath, placed between large bows of hair, and plaits arranged in festoons on the left side, and one single bow of hair on the right, drawn very tight and fastened by a comb. Necklace, ear-rings, and bracelets of gold, ruby, and pearl; long white kid gloves; white satin shoes.

Dinner Dress
June 1826

DINNER DRESS

Dress of Pomona green *gros de Naples*; the *corsage* made moderately high and slightly full in back and front, and ornamented with folds of shaded grenadine, which diverge from a cameo in the centre of the *crèpe lisse* tucker, pass across the bust, and meet in a bow behind. The sleeves are short and rather full, with sleeves *en gigot* in white *crèpe lisse* over them, which are confined at the wrist with tartan bead bracelets, fastened by a cameo. The skirt has two rows of fluted lozenges in shaded grenadine; the longitudinal points connected by a broad flat band of gold-coloured grenadine: beneath is a broad wadded hem or rouleau. The head-dress is very large, and composed of shaded *barège* or grenadine, with a profusion of white ostrich feathers on the left side. The hair parted in front, and arranged in large curls. Gold ear-rings *à la Flamande*; gold chain and necklace. Circular reticule of *ponceau* velvet, edged with gold, and trimmed with British lace; strings of *ponceau* and white satin. Short white gloves; white satin shoes; painted gauze fan.

Ball Dress
June 1826

BALL DRESS

White tulle dress worn over a "Haïti blue" satin slip; the *corsage* high across the bust, very full, and set in a band; the sleeve short and full, with a wreath of China roses down the centre, from the shoulder to the band round the arm. The skirt is decorated with cornucopias of blue and white satin, and a wreath of flowers, emanating from the top of each, falls gracefully, and unites with the point of the next cornucopia: a full puffing of tulle, over a rouleau of blue satin, terminates the edge of the dress. *Ceinture* of Haïti blue; the ends long, the one of white, the other of blue satin ribbon, entwined, and brought across to the opposite side, just above the border, and fastened with a bow and end of each. Head-dress of blue gauze *lisse*; a bow on the right side, confined by a broad plait of hair, which passes behind a small chaplet of roses, placed rather forward on the head: the hair in large curls. Pagoda ear-rings of highly wrought gold; necklace and bracelets of the same; the latter outside the gloves, which are long and of white kid. Grenadine scarf; white satin shoes.

136

Walking Dress
July 1826

WALKING DRESS

Pelisse of straw-colour *gros de Naples*, fastened in front; the collar low, but rather deeper, and projecting as it reaches the back, admitting a narrow ruche of fine tulle: the waist is long and drawn behind, but made to fit the shape in front. The sleeves are large and full to the elbow, whence they gradually lessen, and are finished with a plain neat cuff. The skirt is trimmed down the front with the same material by a continuation of scrolls, enlarging as they descend, attached on the outside by buttons, and within united by their circular termination. The effect is very pleasing. Pelerine or *fichu* of straw-colour *gros de Naples* like the pelisse, trimmed with a double ruche; narrow at the *ceinture*, and expanding towards the shoulders. Hat of straw-colour gros de Naples; the brim large, circular, and flat in front, but shallow behind, ornamented with rays of royal purple ribbon, and a bow at the edge on the left side; the strings uncut; the crown rather high, fully and fancifully trimmed on the right side with broad purple and straw-colour ribbon. *Cornette* of tulle; the hair in large curls; red cornelian brooch, ear-rings, and bracelets. Gloves of pale blue kid; geranium-colour shoes; pale rose-colour parasol, with a white border.

Evening Dress
July 1826

EVENING DRESS

Dress of white *satin Turque*; the *corsage* cut bias, plain and close to the shape, made rather high and circular, and ornamented with a pale blue satin trimming, having very deep scollops corded at the edge; between each scollop is a gold-colour satin piping. The sleeve is very short, moderately full, and set in a band, and has a second row of trimming on the shoulder. The skirt has two flounces; the upper headed by a blue satin rouleau, from behind which golden straps proceed at equal distances, fall over, and sustain the deep scollops, and conceal the commencement of the lower row, which reaches half over the wadded hem at the bottom of the skirt: gold-colour satin sash. The hair is in ringlets, and parted in front *à la Vandyke*, with bows of blue satin on each side, just above the ear. Gold chain with an ornamented cross; long pendant gold ear-rings and necklace; cameo bracelets outside the long white kid gloves, which are French trimmed. Shaded grenadine scarf; white satin shoes; painted horn fan.

Promenade Dress
August 1826

PROMENADE DRESS

Dress of azure *gros de Naples;* the *corsage* regularly full in back and front, rather high and confined by a band of the same material round the top; the sleeve full and large to the elbow; it then fits the arm to the wrist, where it is terminated in a neat full cuff set in a band. The skirt has three flounces, tastefully arranged in divisions of three flutings, then plain, then the flutings alternately; beneath is a wadded hem. Embroidered lace pelerine outside the dress, which reaches to the waist behind; the ends in front are much longer, and pointed and confined by the ceinture: it has a falling collar, fastened in front by a cameo brooch. White *gros de Naples* hat, large and open; the crown rather low, with bows of white satin ribbon on each side, and a piece placed obliquely across the front; white satin bows inside at the commencement of the strings, which hang loose to the *ceinture*, where they meet in a bow, and are fastened in front: a deep blond curtain veil is attached to the edge of the brim. The hair is parted and in large curls; blond cap, the border very full. Gold bracelets and ear-rings; yellow gloves; morocco shoes; rose-colour parasol, with a carved ivory stick ornamented with brass.

Evening Dress
August 1826

EVENING DRESS

White *crèpe lisse* worn over a white satin slip; the *corsage* full, and ornamented with a rose-colour satin cape, corded at the edge, very narrow at its conjunction in front, and extending like a zephyr's wing as it reaches the shoulder, where two ornamented scollops unite it with a similar wing or cape behind: the under-sleeve is short and full, and the long full sleeve over it is terminated at the wrist with a white satin Vandyke cuff, and fastened by a broad gold bracelet with a medallion clasp. The skirt has a deep border of rose-colour satin arranged in two rows; the upper ornament is salver-shaped, supporting an oval composed of flat bands, which cross in the centre, like trellis-work; these ovals are united by bands forming an arch, two extending from the top of one oval to the bottom of the next, and from the other side one band passes behind, reaching from the salver-shaped ornament on the upper row to that on the lower: beneath are two broad rose-colour satin rouleaux. The head-dress is a kind of turban, formed of rose-colour bands, interwoven like trellis-work; the crown is long and rather small towards the top, very similar in shape to the Likanian cap. A white *crepe lisse* rouleau, in *bouffants* entwined by rose-colour bands, reaches round it, lessening as it approaches the right side, where an ornament in rose-colour satin, doubled and in large plaits, extends over the ear. The hair in large curls on the left side, and *à la Madonna* on the right; necklace of medallions united by rows of gold beads; ear-rings *à la Flamande*; shaded gauze scarf, fringed; white kid gloves; white satin shoes.

Carriage Costume
September 1826

CARRIAGE COSTUME

High dress of lilac *gros de Naples*, fastened behind; the fulness of the *corsage* brought to the centre in the front and back; the sleeve large and full at the top, but small below the elbow; corded epaulette, divided in the centre, and trimmed with narrow pinked scallops: the cuff is formed by two rows of vandykes pinked, one row pointing upwards, the other extending towards the hand, with a gold bracelet between. The skirt is ornamented with three rows of pinked trimming, of the same material as the dress, emanating from a button that heads each division; widening as they proceed, they take a semicircular direction till they meet, and by their junction form a continuous chain of scollops: beneath is a satin rouleau. Pinked scolloped pelerine of lilac *gros de Naples*, pointed behind, and tied in front with a satin bow of the same colour, and confined at the waist by the *ceinture*. Blond lappet cap; the border extremely full, spreading like a fan, and rather low in front, arranged in deep vandykes or zig-zags on the sides, and adorned with flowers; trimming of the crown in accordance, and a bow of gold and rose-colour shaded gauze ribbon at the top. Gold chain and embossed Grecian cross; long gold ear-rings; yellow gloves and shoes.

Evening Dress
September 1826

EVENING DRESS

White Italian crape dress worn over a gold-colour satin slip; the *corsage* moderately high, and adorned in front with two pinnatifid branches in gold-colour satin, diverging from the centre of the waist to the top of the bust, and terminating beneath a cape of about a quarter of a yard in depth, divided on the shoulder, and trimmed with gold-colour satin piping and narrow blond. The sleeve is short and full, set in regular plaits, and reversed in the band round the arm. The skirt has an elegant border of gold-colour satin pipings, the three upper rows commencing by a satin bow, elevated in the front of the dress, and turned off circularly towards the right side, proceeding in a longitudinal direction till they (the pipings) meet; then gold-colour satin rows and palm-branches are arranged alternately, and beneath are three pipings, as above, equidistant. Large white *crêpe lisse* sleeves are still in favour, and are confined at the wrist by broad Egyptian bracelets. Gold-colour satin sash, with short bows in front, the ends fringed and of different lengths. The hair is parted towards the left temple in large curls, and adorned with a Provins rose in front, and shaded gauze ribbon in puffs at the back. Pear-shaped pearl ear-rings; necklace of medallions united by rows of small pearl; white kid gloves, and white satin shoes. We are indebted to Miss Bayley of No. 14, Charles-street, Middlesex Hospital, for the accompanying tasteful costumes.

142

Head-Dresses
October 1826

HEAD-DRESSES

1. Hat of rice-straw; the breadth of the brim equal in front and sides, but rather shallow behind; bound with green satin ribbon of the colour of the waters of the Nile: on the outside of the edge, and within the brim on the left side, are small branches of the beautiful Peruvian browallia, from which proceed two ribbons as far as the top of the crown on the right side, where they are interrupted by a cluster of browallias; they descend again and go round the crown, thus crossing it four times in front; a smaller branch of browallia is placed on the opposite side: two bows are attached to *les brides*, or strings withinside the brim.

2. Cap of white *crèpe lisse*; the crown, *à la biret*, is flat, large, and circular, ornamented with blue satin rouleaux spreading from the back; the head-piece is straight, trimmed profusely with deep blond lace, a Provins rose, and waving *crèpe lisse* edged with blue satin.

3. French demi-toilette cap of lilac gauze; the crown very full and arranged *en bouffes*; gold-colour shaded gauze ribbon fancifully disposed in front, with full trimmings of lilac gauze, bound with shaded gold-colour gauze; long loose string of the same, terminated with two bows, and a short end fastened sometimes on the opposite side: deep full border of British lace.

4. Bonnet of sprigged rose-colour *gros de Naples*; the brim large and rounded at the sides, ornamented with two rose-colour satin rouleaux and a curtain blond veil more than half-a-quarter deep: behind is a stiffened silk trimming, the brim not extending to the back; the crown is high, and has a waving trimming and a large cluster of arbutus in front, and also at the edge of the brim, from whence proceeds a rose-colour *crèpe lisse* to the opposite side of the crown, the top of which is arranged in waving flutes, and at the edge is a shell-like ornament: the strings commence with bows on the outside of the brim.

Evening Dress
October 1826

EVENING DRESS

Dress of *gros de Naples*; the colour *acajou*, now much in favour at Paris, that and yellow dividing their empire among the *haut-ton*; the corsage cut bias, and made plain, high across the front and lower on the shoulders, which have epaulettes of puffed ribbon and leaves, uniting with the trimming, that descends on each side of the bust to the sash, which is of the same colour as the dress, and tied behind in two short bows and ends. The sleeves are of a basket form; the upper half plain and projecting; the lower has reversed plaitings, confined to the size of the arm by a band edged with blond. The skirt is ornamented with a rich blond lace nearly a quarter of a yard in depth, set on very full, and headed by a wreath of diamond-shaped leaves, united by a berry and two rouleaux: beneath is a wreath of leaves and wadded hem. The hair is in large curls in front, dressed high, and with large bows at the top; between is a papilionaceous wreath of azure *crèpe lisse*, with gold ornaments. Necklace, ear-rings, and bracelets of embossed gold and beryl; long white kid gloves, trimmed with blond; white satin shoes.

Promenade Dress
November 1826

PROMENADE DRESS

Wadded pelisse of *gros de Naples*, the colour of the blossoms of the pomegranate, made quite plain and to fit the shape, fastened down the front, and ornamented on each side with a row of leaves of an obovate shape; the ends point outwards; they are corded all round, and arranged one beneath the other, and are smaller at the waist, where they approximate, and over the bust, but enlarge as they descend, turn off circularly, and form a border to the skirt, which is terminated by a wadded hem. The sleeve is rather large at the shoulder, but afterwards decreases to nearly the size of the arm, and is finished with a cuff reaching over the hand, and ornamented with obovate leaves pointing upwards. Circular gauze cape, hemmed and edged with a narrow ruche of tulle. Hat of azure gros de Naples, trimmed profusely with blond artificial flowers and shaded ribbon; *les brides*, of shaded blue and gold-colour ribbon, reach below the waist. The hair is parted in front, and displays a narrow border of blond lace; three or four large curls on each side, with bows of blue and gold-colour shaded ribbon. Long coral ear-rings; gold chain and cross, and gold bracelets; yellow gloves and bronze shoes.

Evening Dress
November 1826

EVENING DRESS

Dress of white *crèpe lisse* over a corn-flower blue satin slip; the *corsage* made very full and high in front, with a straight cape, which is divided angularly on the shoulders, and ornamented with a blue satin rouleau. Short and full sleeves beneath the upper long ones, which are spacious to the wrist, where they are terminated with vandyke cuffs, and fastened with broad gold bracelets. The skirt is trimmed with three deep flounces of blond lace, set on very full, and tastefully drawn up in festoons, about half the depth of the lace, by a blue satin rouleau, arranged in a waving direction and confined by buttons placed at regular distances: these flounces are headed by a wreath of leaves *à la antique*; the hem of the slip appears below the dress. Blue satin sash, *à la Francois*, extending from the waist, where it meets in a point, to the shoulders diagonally; it ties in front in two short bows, the ends fringed and reaching half-way down the skirt: bows ornament the shoulder. The head-dress is composed of bows of blue Italian crape, and three very large bows of hair on each side of the crape bow in front; plaited blands of hair are brought from the temples and intersect the bows. Pear-shaped gold ear-rings; gold chain twice round the neck, and an enameled locket pendant in the centre; white kid gloves; white satin shoes.

146

Morning Dress
December 1826

MORNING DRESS

Dress of pale green *ducape;* the *corsage* full, and ornamented round the bust with three rows of deep vandykes of the same material as the dress, headed by a satin rouleau of the same colour; *gigot* sleeve of jaconot muslin, with four bands of green *ducape* equidistant round the lower part of the arm, and confined at the wrist by a gold clasp. The skirt has three deep flounces composed of triangular pieces of *ducape*, with a plait in each: as they extend partly one over the other, they form a very neat and pretty trimming; each row is headed by an indented imbricated satin rouleau. Tucker of tulle, drawn at the top. Cap of tulle; border of scolloped blond lace arranged in the form of two crescents, crossing in front, and continued extremely full in zig-zags on the sides. A garland of leaves is placed above, surrounding the crown, which is full, and ornamented with scolloped blond lace. Ear-rings and necklace of embossed gold; yellow gloves and shoes.

Evening Dress
December 1826

EVENING DRESS

Crimson velvet dress; the *corsage* made plain and rather high, being half a finger's length on the shoulder; seven folded bands of velvet are placed perpendicularly, and form a stomacher reaching below the waist, the centre band forming the point, the others gradually shortening, and the outer band on each side extending over the shoulders and ornamenting the back. The sleeves are short and slashed, admitting very full puffings of white satin; broad velvet band round the arm. The border of the skirt is composed of two rows, of a Gothic pattern, of white *crèpe lisse*, very full, and edged with a corded satin. Crimson satin sash beneath the stomacher, and tied behind in short bows with long ends. The hair is in large curls, and the head-dress composed of blond, arranged *en serpentant*, and artificial flowers. The necklace of gold, with pendant ornaments of different-coloured stones; bracelets and ear-rings *en suite*; Cashmere shawl, white kid gloves, and white satin shoes.

The above elegant costume is from Miss Bayley.

Promenade Dress
January 1827

PROMENADE DRESS

High dress of striped *gros de Naples*, wadded and lined with scarlet sarsnet; the corsage made up to the throat, the straight way of the silk, with a little fulness towards the waist, which is rather long, and confined by a rich plaid scarf, worn as a sash, and tied in front, the ends reaching towards the border of the skirt, which is an horizontal fan-like trimming of scarlet corded point, and is crossed in the centre by longitudinal green velvet fluted puffs; their terminations united by circlets of scarlet satin and green velvet: beneath is a row of chinchilla fur, about half a quarter deep. The sleeves are *en gigot*, and stiffened to keep them extended; they are confined at the wrist by a scarlet corded satin band, fastened with a gold snap: a vandyke cuff extends a little way over the hand, and a second corded band regulates the fulness between the elbow and the wrist: chinchilla fur adorns the shoulders and surrounds the throat. Bonnet of the same material as the dress; the brim circular, edged with a rouleau, and lined with scarlet satin. The crown is almost concealed by its decorations, consisting of three handsome hydrangeas and several large green velvet leaves, besides bows of *gros de Naples*, which are placed on the left side. The hair is dressed in a double row of large curls; the ear-rings are long and of coral; yellow gloves lined with fur; chinchilla muff; and boots of slate-colour morocco.

Wedding Dress
January 1827

WEDDING DRESS

Frock of Urling's sprigged lace, of a very elegant Brussels pattern; the flowers are of an equal size and distance, except on each side, where they are formed into large clusters, and arranged one beneath the other from the waist to the flounce. The *corsage* is circular and of a moderate height, made plain in front, but rather full behind, and has a double row of falling lace of the same rich pattern, but not so deep as the flounce on the skirt. The sleeve is very full, and regulated by seven or eight drawings from the shoulder to below the elbow, from whence it is continued plain to the wrist, where a scolloped cuff graces the hand, corresponding to the scollops at the edge of the dress, which appears just below the flounce. Broad white satin sash, with bows on the right side; white satin slip, with a wadded hem at bottom. The hair is parted in front, and has three very large curls on the left side; above are bows of white satin and *crèpe lisse*: sprigs of myrtle and two full-blown white roses adorn the right side. The necklace consists of three rows of pearl, clasped in front by a brilliant gem; long pearl ear-rings; cameo bracelets. The left arm has an additional bracelet, composed of rows of pearl, united by emeralds. White kid gloves; white satin shoes.

Opera Dress
February 1827

OPERA DRESS

Dress of black crape over lavender satin; the *corsage* made quite plain and moderately high, with a trimming of black Italian crape folded longitudinally à la Farinet, and confined in the centre by a loop, with corded *gros de Naples* edges; the waist rather long; *gigot* sleeves, with an antique cuff of crape, with *gros de Naples* rouleaux, extending from the wrist upwards. The skirt has a deep border of crape, with loops of a black satin semicircular form, with corded edges, arranged four in a perpendicular row, and headed by a corded bow; between each row, which is about a quarter of a yard apart, another bow is introduced; beneath is a wadded hem. Black velvet cloak, made very long and full, and lined with Turkish satin; deep circular cape and square collar. Opera hat, *à la Berri*, of black velvet, the crown fitting close to the head, with an embroidered band; the brim, which is large and circular, is placed above, and ornamented on the right side with a cord and tassels. Gold ear-rings, necklace, and bracelets; white kid gloves, and black kid shoes.

Evening Dress
February 1827

EVENING DRESS

Dress of black *gros de Naples*; the *corsage* cut bias and made with a little fulness, rather high in front, and straight; ornamented with a fluted trimming of black Italian crape, narrow in front, and gradually deepening to the shoulder: the short sleeve is full, and set in a band round the arm; the long sleeve is large, and of crape, with a coronet cuff of *gros de Naples*, fastened by a wrought iron cameo clasp. The skirt is ornamented with an intermixture of *gros de Naples* and crape of a fanciful pattern, headed by a narrow rouleau of satin, which is repeated between the trimming, and the skirt is terminated by a wadded hem. The head-dress consists of a very full wreath of black crape flowers, and a light *crèpe lisse* hat, *à la Marie Stuart*, with long lappets reaching to the waist. Large diamond-shaped black brooch in the front of the bust; German cast-iron necklace, ear-rings, and bracelets with cameo clasps. Black kid gloves and chamois shoes.

Morning Dress
March 1827

MORNING DRESS

Dress of jaconot muslin; the *corsage* made to fit the shape, and ornamented on each side with two rouleaux of lavender-colour satin, approximating at the waist, and spreading like a stomacher towards the shoulder: bows of the same colour adorn the front of the dress; two are placed above the *ceinture*, and six below, at equal distances. The hem at the bottom of the dress has a broad satin ribbon drawn through it. Tucker of blond, drawn close at the top, and tied behind with narrow ribbon. The sleeves are *en gigot*, and have two satin rouleaux extending from a bow on the shoulder to the wrist, and are intercepted by a second bow at the elbow. Gold bracelets, with amethyst clasps, confine the sleeves. The cap, partaking of the turban form, is of tulle, without any border; a band of lavender-colour satin goes round the head, and stiffened bands of satin support the tulle, which is open in front, and contains flowers: the strings are broad and of lavender-colour gauze ribbon. Ear-rings of amethysts. Gloves and shoes of lavender-colour kid.

Evening Dress
March 1827

EVENING DRESS

Dress of white *crèpe lisse*, over a lavender-colour Turkish satin slip; the *corsage* is full, and the waist long; the sleeves are in the Chinese taste, and are formed of four divisions, with projecting points halfway, edged with lavender-coloured satin, and terminating round the arm with a broad satin band, edged with narrow blond: tucker of the same. The skirt is decorated with three rows of the same material as the dress, ornamented with small lavender-colour satin rouleaux, *en car-reaux*, and large roses of emarginate satin leaves, with *crèpe lisse* centres; beneath is a rouleau of satin. Sicilian gauze scarf; lavender-colour sash tied behind in short bows and long ends. The hair is dressed in large curls, and the head-dress composed of a wreath of roses and large bows of lavender-colour Italian crape; embossed gold pagoda ear-rings, and necklace with a cameo locket. Gold bracelets, with cameo clasps outside the gloves, which are of white kid. White satin shoes.

Carriage Costume
April 1827

CARRIAGE COSTUME

Pelisse of primrose *gros de Naples*, or lutestring, lined with white sarsnet; the corsage plain, fastened behind and ornamented with two rows of crescents interlaced, the points projecting outwards. The same kind of trimming is continued down the front of the skirt, and nearly meets at the waist, but widens and enlarges as it descends; it turns off circularly and forms the border of the dress: a rouleau, raised in front and formed into an extended bow, fills the intermediate space and unites with the crescent trimming; the ends of the bow continue all round, beneath the border, and a wadded rouleau hem terminates the dress. The sleeves, of the same material, are long and easy, with large white tulle sleeves over them, confined at the wrist by bead bracelets, with cameo clasps. Vandyked pelerine of tulle, the ends extending below the waist and confined by the *ceinture* in front. Large Mexican hat of lavender and primrose *gros de Nales;* the crown low, and ornamented with ribbons of each colour and large white ostrich-feathers. The strings, one of primrose, the other of lavender-colour ribbon, are untied, and reach nearly to the knees, and have each two bows at the end. The hair, parted on the forehead, is in large curls, with two beautiful Provins roses on each side. Ear-rings and necklace of emerald and gold, fastened very tastefully with a locket pending from the centre; gold watch and chain. Lavender-colour gloves and shoes.

155

Ball Dress
April 1827

BALL DRESS

Dress of rose-colour *crèpe lisse* over a white satin slip; the *corsage* full, rather high in front, and edged with an entwined narrow rouleau, beneath a blonde tucker. The sleeves are short, and set in a rose-colour satin band, and partly encased by tulip-leaves, forming a kind of calyx. The skirt has three rows of graduated satin leaves, each division forming a cone, the top commencing with a diamond-shaped leaf, then a ring of satin, then tulip-leaves; a small double satin rouleau follows, and heads the next row of tulip-leaves, which are larger than those above and smaller than those beneath. The whole is finished by a large satin rouleau, and forms a new and elegant trimming. Rose-colour satin sash, tied behind. The hair in large curls in front, with ringlets on each side behind the ears. Long white kid gloves, trimmed with a quilling of tulle at the top. Gold ear-rings, bracelets, and necklace, with emerald clasps. Rose-colour embroidered satin shoes.

Dinner Dress
May 1827

DINNER DRESS

Dress of white *gros de Naples*; the *corsage* cut bias, and trimmed with *crèpe lisse* in small folds from the top of the bust to the waist. Short full sleeves of *gros de Naples*, with long ones over them of *crèpe lisse*, but not so full as have been worn, confined at the wrist by gold filigree bracelets, with cameo clasps. The shoulders are ornamented by a cruciform bow of gold-colour satin ribbon, from which two pipings of the same colour extend, one forward, the other backward, and are each terminated by a small triangular bow. Tucker of blond, attached to the dress by a gold-colour satin rouleau. The skirt has a deep border of very full *crèpe lisse*, in large puffs, ornamented with cruciform bows placed at regular distances, every two being united by gold-colour satin pipings, which, passing one within the other just above the *crèpe lisse*, seem pending from a bow beyond. Broad rouleau at the bottom of the dress. Gold-colour satin sash. The head-dress consists of a gold-colour satin close or skull cap, pointed in front, and edged with a single row of pearls: large double plaits of gold-colour *crèpe lisse*, stiffened and edged with a narrow band of white satin, surround the head like rays; and behind is a long ornament of platted ribbon, terminating in a bow similar to the net worn by the Neapolitans to contain the hair. Ear-rings, necklace, and cross of amethysts. White kid gloves, and wite satin shoes.

157

Evening Dress
May 1827

EVENING DRESS

Turkish satin dress of pale blue; the *corsage* made close to the shape, and trimmed round the bust with embroidered blond; shallow in front, but deep and full on the shoulders and back. The sleeves are short, and composed of perpendicular rows of blond set in a blue satin band round the arm. The skirt has a very deep flounce of scolloped blond lace of a new and elegant pattern, headed by an open diamond-shape satin trimming, with a band passing longitudinally through each space, and forming a St. Andrew's cross at every change. Beneath the flounce are narrow rouleaux entwined. The head-dress is a toque of garter-blue satin, with a train band of various coloured stones. Three ostrich-feathers are placed in front, and two, falling very low, on each side. The ear-rings, necklace, and bracelets are of filigree gold, with medallions of different coloured stones. Gold chain and eye-glass, watch, chain, and trinkets. White kid gloves, trimmed; white satin shoes.

Promenade Dress
June 1827

PROMENADE DRESS

Pelisse of lavender-colour watered *gros de Naples*; the *corsage* has a little fulness behind at the waist, but is made close to the shape in front, though nut so high as the throat, being rather open, and displaying a full chemisette of French cambric, with a square worked collarette falling over. The pelisse fastens in front with hooks and eyes, and is decorated with bows; a broad band, edged with satin of the same colour, descends from the waist, goes round and forms the border of the pelisse, and is ornamented by a row of painted leaves, with rouleau satin binding, which is continued over the bust and meets behind. The sleeves are *en gigot*, and have broad waistbands, with printed leaves to correspond: *ceinture* edged with satin. Rose-colour hat of watered *gros de Naples*; the brim extremely large, with a blond curtain veil, a quarter of a yard deep; the crown circular, and the trimming in the form of large leaves, with rose-colour satin rouleau binding, and a bouquet of flowers on each side: the strings are of broad satin ribbon, and descend from a bow on the left side; they are very long and untied, and have each a bow at the end. Gold ear-rings, chain and cross; yellow gloves; black kid shoes.

159

Evening Dress
June 1827

EVENING DRESS

Dress of white tulle over a white satin slip, made straight across the bust, a little full in front, and rather low on the shoulder. The sleeves are short and ornamented with puffs in the form of cordatum, or heart-shaped leaves of tulle, surrounded by a band of white satin, edged on each side with gold-colour satin, and fastened at the points with small buttons. Narrow trimming of blond round the arm and top of the *corsage*: two bands of gold-colour satin are arranged on each side from the shoulder to the front of the waist, where they are crossed by the ceinture which is fastened by a ruby clasp with a pendant pear-shaped pearl. Three bands descend from the waist half way down the skirt, and support three cordata puffs, similar, though larger than those on the sleeves; these rest on four beneath, which are placed on the points of five more, which belong to the border that surrounds the dress: a broad white satin band, ornamented with spots of gold-colour satin, between transverse bands of the same and a narrow rouleau, terminates the dress. The head-dress consists of a gold tiara comb adorned with different coloured oval stones, and an embroidered veil of tulle, arranged in two large bows on the crown of the head, and falling in graceful drapery over the shoulders. The hair is parted on the forehead and in large curls on each side; it is dressed very high at the top between the comb and the veil. Earrings, necklace, and locket of filigree gold, studded with rubies; gold bracelets with ruby clasps outside the gloves, which are of white kid, and drawn at the elbow with gold-colour satin ribbon; white satin shoes.

160

Carriage Costume
July 1827

CARRIAGE COSTUME

Missolonghi dress of grass-green silk *barège*, with an elegant shawl pattern border, of various colours, and nearly half a yard deep: beneath is a flounce of grass-green *crèpe lisse*, arranged in festoons. The *corsage* has a little fulness, and is straight across the bust; the sleeves are *en gigot*, with two rows of shawl-pattern scollopped trimmings on the shoulders. Pelisse of *tulle*, with a white satin cording and scolloped blonde lace at the edge; full behind, and terminating at the waist, but extending below the *ceinture* in front; standing-up collar, confined by a ribbon of royal purple and gold slider, ornamented amulet cross suspended, reaching to the waist. White *gros de Naples* Spanish hat; the brim very large, turned up and slashed all round, the interstices filled up with green *crèpe lisse*, headed by rose-colour satin buttons. On the right side of the crown are placed some bell-shaped feather-flowers, and a plume of pink and white ostrich-feathers, which fall over the front of the hat. The hair is parted from the forehead, and in ringlets on each side. Gold filigree ear-rings and bracelets; silk *barège* azure scarf; yellow gloves and shoes.

Ball Dress
July 1827

BALL DRESS

Frock of white *crêpe lisse* over a rose-colour satin slip: the *corsage* is full, and ornamented with pendant bows or loops of rose-colour gauze ribbon. The sleeves are short and full, confined by a rose-colour satin band round the arm, and the shoulders decorated with epaulettes formed of loops similar to those that adorn the bust, only larger. The skirt has a very deep and full puffing of *crêpe lisse*, tastefully trimmed with moss-roses attached to loops of rose-colour gauze ribbon, arranged pyramidally, and alternately placed at the upper and lower edges of the puffing; rose-colour satin rouleau beneath. Shaded rose-colour gauze sash, fastened by an embossed gold buckle on the left side without bows, but having three ends of different lengths, each terminated with a double bow. The hair is dressed in curls in front, with a plain and a plaited band above, and *à la couronne* at top; and *belles du jour* convolvuluses are interspersed. Necklace and ear-rings of Neapolitan or seed-beads, dispersed in a tasteful and novel style. White kid gloves, slashed at the top and admitting pink satin ribbon, which ties in a small bow. Bracelets formed of two chains of twisted gold, and fastened by a white cornelian clasp. Parisian gold chain, and eye-glass. White satin shoes.

Promenade Dress
August 1827

PROMENADE DRESS

Gros de Naples dress of fawn colour, made high and easy, with a little fulness in the centre of the front and back set in, in the band round the waist. The sleeves are large and full, and fastened at the wrist by black velvet bracelets, with amulet clasps. The skirt is ornamented with a broad ribbon, *en carrè*, of the same colour, above a deep flounce, with small scollops at the edge, pinked; the ribbon, *en carrè*, is repeated, and beneath is a drapery spread out at the top and bottom like a fan, drawn together in the centre, and confined by a bow. Large circular vandyked *collerette* of French cambric, beautifully worked, and tied at the throat with azure gauze ribbon; the ends are very long, and each terminated by a bow: worked vandyke cuffs of French cambric. Hat of azure *gros de Naples*, crossed with yellow and purple; it is large and open in front, displaying the hair, which is very tastefully arranged in large curls: the strings are, one of rose colour, the other of azure, and confine the hat close to the chin: the crown is rather low, and decorated with Peruvian browallias and passion-flowers, and ribbons of azure and rose-colour. Gloves and shoes of blue kid.

163

Evening Dress
August 1827

EVENING DRESS

Dress of white crape over a white satin slip; the *corsage* is made slightly full and rather high, with a narrow tucker of folded *crèpe lisse*. The sleeves are extremely short and full, and ornamented with three serpentine scrolls, formed of oval rose-colour puffs, large at the shoulder, where they commence, and gradually decreasing to a point. The front of the dress is decorated by three wreaths of rose-colour laurel-leaves, beginning at the row of leaves that surrounds the top of the bust; they approximate at the waist, extend and rather enlarge as they descend, and form the upper part of the border of the skirt. The centre wreath passes beneath, and unites the base of the serpentine ornaments, formed of oval puffs placed together as on the sleeve, only considerably larger; the centre scrolls meet in an elegant form in front, and are united by a fancy cross; small circular spots are dispersed between the laurel and about the border: the skirt is terminated by a double row of vandyke rose-colour satin. The head-dress is composed of alternate bows of gold tissue and crimson ribbon on the left side; a comb richly adorned with coloured stones in front, where a bird of Paradise inserts its beak, and its beautiful plumage falls gracefully over the right side; bows of ribbon are then placed more forward, and a lace veil descends in elegant drapery from the back of the head. Gold ear-rings, chain, and eye-glass; white cornelian necklace, entwined with gold; broad gold bracelets set with rubies; white kid gloves; white satin shoes.

164

Sea-Side Costume
September 1827

SEA-SIDE COSTUME

Dress of canary-colour *gros de Naples*, with narrow stripes; the *corsage* made full and rather high. The skirt has two deep flounces, of the same material as the dress; the lower set on straight, and very full; the upper in four festoons, the elevations being in front, at the sides and back: the flounces are each headed by a flat band of canary-colour *gros de Naples*, edged with orange-colour satin rouleaus. Pelerine of the same, drawn behind, slashed on the shoulders, and extending below the *ceinture* in front, by which it is confined: it is ornamented by a band, edged on each side with orange-colour satin, corresponding with the *ceinture*, &c; *gigot* sleeves of plain jaconot muslin, fastened at the wrist with black velvet bracelets. Circular embroidered *collerette*, tied with canary-colour ribbon. British Leghorn hat; the brim very large and circular, and ornamented within side, near the edge, by a rouleau of lilac *crèpe lisse*, entwined with canary-colour satin ribbon; the crown rather low, and decorated with large feather-flowers, puffs of lilac *crèpe lisse*, and twisted rouleau, as beneath the brim: lilac strings tied on the left side. Lilac kid gloves; yellow morocco shoes.

165

Evening Dress
September 1827

EVENING DRESS

Dress of white crape over a white satin slip; rose-colour satin bodice made close to the shape and formed like a stomacher; narrow shoulder-straps of rose-colour satin, and Farinet tucker of folded *crépe lisse*, fastened in front by an antique gem; gigot sleeves of white crape, with deep cuffs of rose-colour satin, the upper part scolloped with rouleau binding, and that next the hand embroidered with a wreath of the same colour. The skirt is not gored, but full in front and at the sides, though the principal fulness is placed behind; has a deep border of rose-colour satin, scolloped at the top and terminated with a slightly wadded hem; above is a row of alternate satin stars and roses. Large circular dress hat of rose-colour crape, with satin rouleau binding of the same colour placed rather on one side, looped up in front with folded white crape, and confining some flowers that peep through and mingle with the hair, which is arranged in large curls. The crown has a garland of flowers, very numerous in front, and resting on the edge of the brim. Chinese ear-rings; necklace and bracelets of rice, of curious workmanship; white kid gloves; white satin shoes; circular shaded feather fan.

Promenade Dress
October 1827

PROMENADE DRESS

Dress of Egyptian blue *du Cape*, made high and very full; the sleeves en gigot; the skirts sufficiently long to touch the ground behind, and ornamented by straps with satin rouleau edges of the same colour; they are pointed at the top and formed into triangles by rouleaus beneath, from which they descend as low as the hem, terminating broad. Tulle pelisse, with three vandykes on the shoulders forming epaulettes, edged with gold-colour satin, tied at the throat with ribbon of the same colour, and confined at the waist by a band of Egyptian blue *du Cape*, fastened in front with a plain gold buckle; *collerette* of tulle, vandyked and edged with gold-colour satin. Close bonnet of floss silk; the colour graduated from deep orange to pale straw; lined with pale pink satin, and ornamented with shaded ostrich feathers; strings *en bride*. Embroidered lace veil; gold bracelets and ear-rings; corded silk boots, with a narrow fringe at the top; yellow gloves.

Ball Dress
October 1827

BALL DRESS

Dress of white tulle over a white satin slip; the sleeves are made short and full, confined round the arm by a straw-colour satin band, and ornamented with bows and ends, of the same colour, reaching below the sleeve. The *corsage* is plain, with a very full falling trimming of blond round the top, which is circular and rather high. The skirt is decorated with deep festoons of straw-colour satin, commencing by two bows and surmounted by a tripartite ornament; beneath are two small satin rouleaus, distant the width of the hem, and shewing the transparent tulle between: sash of straw-colour satin, with bows and long ends on each side and behind. The hair is dressed in large curls, with plaited bands, arranged between a garland of blue dahlias. Close to the throat is a delicate gold chain, entwined three or four times, and beneath is a row of small pearl set in gold, with pear-shaped pearls pendant; ear-rings to correspond. On the left arm is an elegant armlet of coloured stones in embossed gold; Neapolitan bead bracelets outside the white kid gloves, which are stamped and drawn at the elbow; gold tissue shoes; Jocko cedar fan.

Morning Dress
November 1827

MORNING DRESS

Pomeguanate-colour *gros de Naples* dress, checked with black and a deeper shade of pomegranate; the body is made high and full, and the sleeves *en gigot*; the skirt has a little fulness in front, and is trimmed with three deep bias tucks, the upper not so broad as the two lower. Vandyked tulle pelerine, with falling circular collar, edged with white satin, and meeting just above the waist. The vandykes are progressively large to the shoulder, where they are very deep, and lessen again towards the back. Sprigged lace cap, placed rather forward; the border broad and full, with cross-barred blue gauze ribbon between the spaces in front: above the border the ribbon is plain as far as the temple, from whence it is pressed round the back part of the cap: the crown is full and regulated by blue ribbon. The hair is dressed in ringlets. Plain gold earrings; eye-glass suspended by a black ribbon formed into a loop, and confined at the throat by a gold filigree slider, ornamented with rubies. Black velvet bracelets and sash, with short bows and pointed ends, reaching to the tucks of the dress in front; blue kid gloves; black shoes of *gros des Indes*.

Dinner Dress
November 1827

DINNER DRESS

White tulle dress over a Tyrian blue satin slip, with short full sleeves. The waist is long and the body full, and trimmed with a falling scollopped blond lace round the top, which is circular and rather high; the sleeves are large, terminated by a double trimming, and confined at the wrists with gold bracelets, with white cornelian cameo clasps. The skirt is decorated by a festoon of embroidered tulle, with a blue satin rosette at each elevation; beneath is a narrow satin rouleau of the same colour, heading a very deep and beautifully embroidered flounce. Blue satin sash, edged and spotted with gold-colour; bows and ends on the left side. Toque of Tyrian blue satin and white *crépe lisse*, adorned with gold lace, and a broad band of the same round the head. Necklace of white pearl and turquoise, with an ornamented crescent pendant from the centre: ear-rings to correspond. White gauze scarf, with longitudinal rows of gold-colour satin; white kid gloves; blue satin shoes.

Carriage Dress
December 1827

CARRIAGE DRESS

High dress of green Merino, with *gigot* sleeves and broad wristbands, fastened with hooks and eyes, and confining the gloves, which are of rose-colour kid; the skirt is trimmed with two deep flounces of the same material as the dress, headed and edged with a shawl pattern border of roses. Cloak of tomata-colour *gros de Berlin*, lined with ermine, made very long and full, and drawn at the waist behind; the arm-holes are bound with tomata-colour velvet, like the large circular cape, which is fastened in front with a gold clasp *a la militaire*; square collar, falling over and displaying the ermine lining. Blue silk Navarino hand- kerchief tied round the throat. White *gros de Naples* hat, with a wide and spreading brim, ornamented beneath with rows of tomata-colour satin ribbon, on each side united by a ribbon extending across the front; the crown is decorated with white and tomata-colour satin trimming, and white ostrich feathers disposed in front and at the sides; satin strings *en bride*. Muff of ermine, and shoes of dark chesnut-colour kid.

Ball Dress
December 1827

BALL DRESS

Crépe lisse dress over a white satin slip; the sleeves are very short and full, and terminated with a wreath of china roses and deep vandykes, edged with a narrow ruche of tulle; Spanish bodice of rose-colour satin, laced in front as a stomacher with silver cord, vandyked at the waist, and trimmed with silver lace. The skirt is decorated with a wreath of full-blown Provins roses, about half a yard above the rose-colour satin rouleau at the edge of the dress, which is supported by loops of rose-colour satin ribbon, having a knot in the centre, and attached to the wreath of roses by the upper loop: in each division is a star embroidered in rose-colour floss silk; sash of the same colour, reaching from the right side across the front, where it is *noué*, and extending transversely to the left side, and fastened to the wreath of roses. The head-dress consists of a garland of red and white camellia Japonica, rising from between two large bows of hair at the top, and extending all round the head, and intermingling with the curls; ornamented gold comb behind. Necklace of gold and turquoise, with a diamond - shape locket in front; delicately wrought gold chain and eye-glass, and pendent gold ear-rings; medallion bracelets outside the white kid gloves; white satin shoes and sandals.

172

Head-Dresses
January 1828

HEAD-DRESSES

1. Hat of *couleur monstre*, or light green striped velvet; the brim, extremely wide and spreading in the front and sides, contains behind half a quarter deep and full, being a continuation of the lower velvet trimming that surrounds the crown, placed low on the left and high on the right side: the trimming on the front above is folded in a picturesque style. Papilionaceous bows of rich satin ribbon, of cherry-colour and black, adorn the left side, and spread from the top of the crown towards the right; three small branches of the golden or Portuguese everlasting fall gracefully from opposite points.

2. Toque of fine tulle spreading upwards from a broad gold band, which has two bows and an end pendant from the right side. The toque is edged at the top with gold lace; the crown is low and full, and has a star in the centre.

3. Turban of crimson velvet, with two ostrich feathers of the same colour on the right side, and a projecting ornament of black velvet, bound with gold lace, on the left; bandeau of ermine.

4. Parisian hat of black velvet, bound with gold-colour satin, and lined with pink; the brim is very large and double in front; two curled ostrich feathers of scarlet and gold emanate from the space between, and one extends beyond the edge of the brim. The crown is made plain, and has a fan-like bow of gold and black satin ribbon, very broad; and a large ostrich feather, attached to the centre, extends in a waving direction towards the right side; strings of gold and black satin ribbon.

Ball Dress
January 1828

BALL DRESS

Crèpe lisse dress of bird of Paradise yellow, with short full sleeves, set in a black satin band round the arm; stomacher front, composed of five perpendicular divisions, widening towards the top of the bust, and displaying black satin puffings between; scollopped blond trimming in front, deepening to a zephyr cape on the shoulders and at the back. The point of the stomacher is low, and finished with a *ruche* of tulle. The skirt is short, and ornamented with three rosaceous borders of the same material as the dress, with black satin puffings at the corners, and is terminated with a yellow satin rouleau: a band of the same colour is arranged between each of the borders. The hair is dressed in large curls in front, high on the top, and ornamented with tulle drapery, and supported with a tiara comb. Necklace, ear-rings, and bracelets of embossed gold and turquoise; white kid gloves; French trimmed gold tissue shoes and sandals.

Promenade Dress
February 1828

PROMENADE DRESS.

Merino high dress of *giraffe* colour; made plain and fastened in front: the waist long, with a broad band of the same material as the dress: *gigot* sleeves, with deep black velvet cuffs, ornamented with gold buttons: circular black velvet cape, trimmed with black lace. The skirt has a border of black velvet, cut bias, and adorned with five gold buttons in front: blue and scarlet silk kerchief, beneath the dress, rises just above the cape, and ties in front.

Circular hat of blue velvet; the crown full; the brim, broad in front and narrow behind, edged and trimmed with *giraffe*-colour velvet; the trimming in front resembling fern in shape: the strings are *en bride*, but not very long. Light blue gloves; *giraffe*-colour shoes; chinchilla muff.

Evening Dress
February 1828

EVENING DRESS

The body of scarlet velvet, made close to the shape, and quite plain; pointed in front, and ornamented with a cruciform bow, and edged with gold lace: circular epaulettes, edged with gold on either side. Farinet tucker, of longitudinal folds of white *crèpe lisse:* sleeves of scarlet velvet, short, full, and stiffened; long sleeves, of white *crèpe lisse*, full to the wrist, where they are terminated by broad gold filigree bracelets, with cameo clasps. The skirt is of white China crape, finished with a broad wadded hem, and ornamented with two flounces of white *crèpe lisse*, cut bias and double, edged with narrow scarlet velvet, and headed by a row of vandykes or *dents de loup*. The hair is parted in front, and arranged tastefully in curls on each side. Coronet shape head-dress of jewels, set in gold and silver gauze. Necklace and ear-rings of filigree gold, adorned with emeralds and pink topazes. Imperial Chinese yellow gauze scarf; while kid gloves, embroidered in the form of a star at the backs, and confined beneath the bracelets; silver tissue shoes.

Dinner Dress
March 1828

DINNER DRESS

White satin dress made with a frock-body, equally full and round, square at the top and ornamented by a cape, straight in front and deep on the shoulders, where it has three pointed divisions: it is trimmed with narrow blond. The sleeves are *en gigot*, and terminated by broad fancy bracelets of garnet and gold. The skirt is decorated by a row of white satin bows, with two angular ends pointing downwards. Beneath is a puffed triangular trimming, united by a rouleau to a deep and full bias flounce that touches the ground. Broad gold belt, embroidered in crimson bows, and long ends, tasselled, attached to the left side. The hair is parted from the forehead, with two curls on each side, and confined by a gold band, beneath a toque of rose-colour *crèpe lisse*. The edge of the brim is rather elevated, slightly constructed, and decorated with broad rose-colour satin ribbon, having bows on each side, beneath the brim, and bows on the low circular crown, with long ends projecting over the edge, on the left side. Gold ear-rings and necklace, with turquoise ornaments. White kid gloves, embroidered with gold *giraffe*-coloured kid shoes.

Ball Dress
March 1828

BALL DRESS

White tulle dress over a Feodore blue satin slip: the waist is long, and pointed at the back and front, and bound with gold lace: the stomacher extends to the top of the shoulder, where it terminates in an obtuse angle, projecting over the sleeves, and united to an angular cape, that decorates the back: a branch of white Persian roses spreads over the front, and gives the stomacher an elegant appearance: it is terminated with a rosaceous ornament of rubies set in gold. The sleeves are short and full, and kept out by the stiffened sleeves of the slip. The skirt is made equally full all round, bound with white satin, open in front, but united at regular distances by five rosaceous ruby clasps set in gold: branches of white Persian roses form its rich and delicate border: it is a quarter of a yard shorter than the slip, which is terminated by a blue satin rouleau. The hair is parted in front, dressed in large bows, and adorned with papilionaceous bows of blue and gold tissue ribbon. White kid gloves; medallion bracelets outside. Earrings à la Flamande; gold necklace, with a diamond-shape locket in front; gauze scarf; white satin shoes.

Carriage Costume
April 1828

CARRIAGE COSTUME

Dress of lilac *gros de Naples*, made rather high, the fulness of the body drawn towards the shoulders: the sleeves are *en gigot*, ornamented with two rows of pendent lilac-leaves stiffened, of the same material as the dress; one row is placed just above the elbow, the other between that and the waist. The skirt is set on full, and trimmed with two deep flounces, each headed by a row of pendent lilac-leaves: satin sash of the same colour. Double pelerine of embroidered tulle; the shape circular, and very deeply vandyked with a stiffened projecting collar, having a rose-colour satin ribbon drawn through it at the top, and tied in front: the bows small, the ends long, reaching to the lower flounce, and terminating in double bows. Cap of tulle; the border of blond, very full, and arranged in large puffs; the crown high, with trimmings of blond, and a large radiated bow of rose-colour satin, placed a little towards the left side. Hair *en grand boucle*. Gold ear-rings and bracelets; white kid gloves; black satin shoes.

Evening Dress
April 1828

EVENING DRESS

Dress of *giraffe*-colour tiffany, painted in waving columns of fancy flowers, and crossed, diagonally by lines of Ionian gray. The waist is long, and the upper part of the body full, terminating in a point in front: the *ceinture*, bound with satin cord, is attached to it, and partakes of the form of a diamond, the longitudinal corners continuing round the waist in a broad band. The sleeves are of white *crèpe lisse*, long and full, confined at the wrist by gold bracelets, and ornamented thence to the elbow by three heraldic roses of pink satin, with green centres. Zephyr cape of *crèpe lisse*, with three narrow pipings of white satin, and fastened in front and at the divisions on the shoulders by oval ornaments of emeralds and gold. The skirt, though full in front and at the sides, has the principal fulness behind, and has a deep border of fluted *crèpe lisse*, decorated with three rows of heraldic roses, in pink satin and green centres, at equal distances one between the other; beneath is a small rouleau of *giraffe*-colour satin.

The hair is dressed in long and large curls around the head, very high at the top, in three large bows, supported by a semicircle of green satin, behind a rosette of rose-colour satin placed just above the division of the hair on the forehead. Gold ear-rings, and delicately wrought gold chain, entwined and passing three of four times round the neck. Short kid gloves, of pale pink, tied at the wrist. *Giraffe*-colour satin shoes.

Promenade Dress
May 1818

PROMENADE DRESS

Pelisse of apple-green *gros de Naples*, closed in front and fastened by gold buckles, with angular straps corded at the edge, of the same material as the pelisse. The body is made close to the shape, almost as high as the throat, and quite plain; *gigot* sleeves, with corded indented triangular cuffs, pointing upwards. The skirt is full at the back and sides, and a small space left plain in front. The border is of chenille *en trellis*, the corners confined by circlets of apple-green satin; broad corded band above, fastened in front by a gold buckle. *Collerette* of French cambric, composed of two rows of pendant straps, embroidered in satin stitch. Large circular hat, of white *gros de Naple,* edged with rose-colour satin, placed rather forward, and displaying a row of curls behind: a plume of rose-colour quadrille feathers adorns the right side, which fall in opposite directions, the end of one extending over the front and left side of the brim, the other drooping backwards; round the corner is a broad rose-colour satin ribbon folded diagonally, and terminating in a long bow beneath the feathers: vvithinside the brim are two bows, from which long lawn strings proceed, ornamented with bows and ends at the extremities. Red cornelian ear-rings and brooch; gold bracelets, with red cornelian clasps; short kid gloves of primrose-colour; black satin Parisian shoes and sandals.

Evening Costume
May 1828

EVENING COSTUME

Dress of cherry-colour crape ariophane, worn over a white satin slip. The body is of cherry-colour satin, made to the form and rather tight, pointed in front, and edged with cord: it is trimmed with longitudinal folds of crape ariophane, ornamented with three cruciform bows of cherry-colour satin ribbon; the back is trimmed in the same manner, and is rather low. Melon sleeves of white crape ariophane, set in a rose-colour satin band, with a projecting pointed leaf rising from the centre. The skirt is made without gores, and is fulled in all round at the waist, and trimmed with a rose-colour satin rouleau, and ornamented by two rows of very full crape, regulated into puffs by rose-colour satin ribbon and a branch of scarlet Fuchsia: the upper row commences half way up the skirt, and turns off in a circular direction towards the back, leaving an open space in front; the opposite side is formed to correspond: the row beneath partakes of the same tasteful direction, nearly touching at its commencement the row above, and reaching to the satin rouleau below. Two bows of rose-colour satin ribbon, with ends of different lengths, are attached to the point of the stomacher or front. The hair is dressed high, and ornamented with a tiara gold and pearl comb on the right side, with long flat bows of hair at the summit, and large bows of blue and rose-colour ariophane crape arranged to give height; the hair is parted on the right temple, and in four large curls on the left. Gold ear-rings, necklace, and bracelets. Gauze scarf of various colours; white kid gloves, with rose-colour embroidered backs; white satin shoes and sandals.

Morning Dress
June 1828

MORNING DRESS

Pale lavender-colour *gros de Naples* high dress; the waist long and pointed in front. The body is cut bias, and sits very close to the shape; a little fulness at the upper part is confined by gold filigree buttons. The sleeves are made plain and large as far as the elbow, but afterwards scarcely exceed the size of the arm. The skirt is set on with nearly an equal fulness all round, and is ornamented with a waving satin piping of the same colour, elevated on the left side, sustaining bells in pairs, about half a quarter of a yard apart. The hat is large and circular, placed rather low on the right side, with a slight declination in front: it is of the same material and colour as the dress, lined with pale pink satin, and ornamented with two large bows of broad gauze and ribbon of various colours, on the top of the crown; the strings proceed from them, and are fastened under the lavender-colour trimming that adorns the crown on each side. Double *collerette* of French cambric, the upper divided into five beautifully worked vandykes; the other square, and worked in small scollops and bouquets, and fastened by a gold filigree buckle in front. Gold ear-rings and jointed onyx bracelets; yellow gloves; black satin shoes.

Ball Dress
June 1828

BALL DRESS

Ariophane crape dress, over a bird of paradise yellow satin slip. The *corsage* is made full and square across the bust, and is ornamented with three longitudinal pipings of yellow satin. The sleeves are short and full, with epaulettes of yellow satin *en coquille*. The skirt is fulled in all round the waist, and terminated with a yellow satin rouleau, and is trimmed half way up with ornaments of a semi-lunar shape, tapering to a point in the curve below, but open at the top, and containing a bouquet of flowers. Gold tissue belt, decorated with a row of buttons arranged perpendicularly from the upper to the lower point. The hair is parted on the right temple, dressed *en grand boucle*, and confined by a pearl bandeau; on the crown of the head are three large bows of hair, bordered by rows of pearls, and supported by long pins, concealed withinside the bows. Gold tiara, and a plume of white ostrich feathers placed at the back of the head; two stand upright, and two long ones drop towards the left shoulder. Parisian gauze scarf; diamond earrings and necklace; mosaic bracelets; white kid gloves, stamped at the top; white satin shoes and sandals.

Morning Dress
July 1828

MORNING DRESS

Dress of *giraffe*-colour baptiste, with small lilac sprigs; the *corsage à l' Espagnol*, rather high and straight across the bust, edged with a narrow cording of lilac *gros de Naples*, and a rouleau of the same down the front and on each side, in the form of a stomacher: it is divided into straps, edged with lilac round the waist, which is of a moderate length. Sontag sleeves, extremely full as far as the elbow, and divided by three lilac *gros de Naples* bands; the rest of the sleeve is shaped to the arm and the wrist ornamented with vandykes. The skirt is gathered full as far as the stomacher, and has a flounce half a yard deep, arranged in large flutes, headed by a *giraffe*-colour band edged with lilac, with semicircular ornaments above, and a waving band, which entwines each division of the flounce; and beneath are two rows of lilac satin, with orange-colour satin of the same width, cut bias, and placed transversely over the lilac. *Giraffe* head-dress; at the top in front are two high bows of hair sustained by pins, and bows of satin and gauze ribbon, interspersed with large curls. Necklace and bracelets of rows of small coral twisted; lilac gloves; black shoes and sandals.

Fancy Ball Dress
July 1828

FANCY BALL DRESS

Sclavonian dress of Tyrian blue gauze, with a broad band of gold tissue on each side of the front, which is a little open, and round the skirt, which is very short; it meets at the waist, and is fastened with a large clasp in the form of a star, composed of rubies in the centre, surrounded by emeralds: the bodice is made close to the shape, and laced in front with rose-colour silk cord, and a trimming of Grecian lace adorns the top of the bust above the gold tissue band. The sleeves are triangular, of white ariophane crape, set in very full on the shoulder, and terminating in a point below the elbow, forming a shell-like receptacle for the arm, open in front, where a rose-colour satin bow is placed, with long ends pendant, finished with gold ornaments. The skirt is slashed on each side of the front from the waist to the border, and bound with narrow gold - colour satin and laced with rose-colour silk, and displaying the white satin slip beneath, which is made with a deep and very full border of Tyrian blue gauze, reaching within three inches of the gold tissue border of the dress: it is ornamented with perpendicular rose-colour satin rouleaus a quarter of a yard apart. The head-dress consists of a fancy turban, having on one side a row of lunulatum-leaves of Tyrian blue satin, edged with gold, and strung on a gold cord; a plume of white ostrich feathers, with a cluster of golden pheasants' feathers, in the centre, on the right side. White cornelian earrings. Necklace of large white cornelian beads, one row close to the throat, a second reaching to the waist. Armlets and bracelets of chain embossed gold, with white cornelian cameo clasps. White kid gloves, embroidered; gold tissue shoes and sandals.

Carriage Costume
August 1828

CARRIAGE COSTUME

Gros de Naples high dress of Pomona green, ornamented with three deep flounces of the same, each having at the top a border of the York and Lancaster rose arranged alternately. The body is made plain, and the waist long: the sleeves are very full, and confined twice above the elbow with rose-colour satin bands, fastened with square gold buckles; beneath the elbow it is made to fit the arm, and is laced above half way, and has a rose-colour cord and tassels pendant: corded rose-colour satin belt, pointed in front, with small bows behind: *ruche* of tulle, and pelerine of the same, scolloped at the back, and reaching to the belt in front. Leghorn hat, circular and large, trimmed with rose-colour satin ribbon and artificial flowers; tied under the right ear in a large bow, and long full ends of rose-colour *crèpe lisse*. Primrose-colour gloves and shoes.

Evening Dress
August 1828

EVENING DRESS

A French white gauze dress over an azure satin slip, with short full stiffened sleeves: the body of the dress is of azure satin, close to the shape, and slopes from the shoulders, where it is very narrow; it laces in front, is open at the top, and gradually closes as a stomacher, and has a cord and tassels attached to the point in front: the tucker is formed of longitudinal folds of white gauze. Long full sleeves, with three azure-corded azure satin bands, each ornamented with a bow in front. The skirt is trimmed above half way by two rows of oblong ornaments, bound by azure satin, and headed by bouquets of roses, placed at each division and united by azure satin: the skirt is terminated with a rouleau of the same. The hair is in ringlets, and ornamented with ostrich feathers; one, tipped with azure, is placed behind several bows of geranium-colour satin ribbon on the right side; another, a *solitaire*, falls low on the left. Gold ear-rings *à la Flamande* ornamented with pearl; fancy gold necklace, with pendant pearls, and broad gold bracelets, with white cameo clasps. White kid gloves, with elastic bands at the wrist. White satin shoes and sandals.

Morning Dress
September 1828

MORNING DRESS

Jaconot muslin dress, made as high as the throat, where it is finished with a narrow band, confining the fulness of the body; a small circular cape, drawn with blue satin ribbon, and trimmed with work half a quarter deep, commences in front of the shoulder and extends across the back: the sleeves are *à la Gabrielle,* being full above the elbow, and below confined by three drawings to the shape of the arm. The skirt is set on with equal fulness all round, and has a flounce half a yard deep, headed by a trimming composed of a rouleau adorned with demi-whorls, made of book muslin, gathered very full, and edged with blue braiding; a second whorl trimming divides the flounce half way: blue satin cestus, pointed in front. Provincial French cap of tulle made of one piece, and drawn full round the head: it is greatly elevated, and falls back from the summit in two divisions like lappets, the ends trimmed with blond lace, and reaching as low as the shoulder: bows of blue satin ribbon are tastefully dispersed; and the border, being very full, forms a rosette in front, and bows of blue satin ribbon intermingle with the curls of hair round the face. Ear-rings and necklace of rock coral; broad Grecian scroll bracelets of gold. Rose-colour gloves; blue corded silk shoes.

Evening Dress
September 1828

EVENING DRESS

Rose-colour *gros de Naples* dress; the waist long, and pointed in the front and back, and trimmed with a narrow *ruche* of tulle round the top of the bust: the sleeves are *à la Marie Stuart;* the upper part being very full, and twice divided by a rose-colour satin band round the arm, and terminated at the wrist by a deep cuff, with vandykes pointing towards the elbow. The skirt is made without gores, very full and plaited in all round the waist, and is ornamented with a *ruche* of tulle and a very deep flounce of Chatillon sprigged blond lace, placed about half-way of the skirt, and falls within a finger's length of the wadded hem, which touches the ground. The hair is parted in front, and dressed in light and becoming curls on the side and behind. Spanish hat of rose-colour satin, the brim a little turned up on the sides, and a slight declination in front; the crown is low, and adorned with a profusion of white ostrich feathers, fastened by a pink topaz star. Gold necklace and ear-rings; the latter in the form of a leaf and bunch of grapes; vinegarette suspended from a Chinese chain; broad chain bracelet, with circular emerald snaps. Embroidered gauze scarf; white kid gloves; white satin shoes.

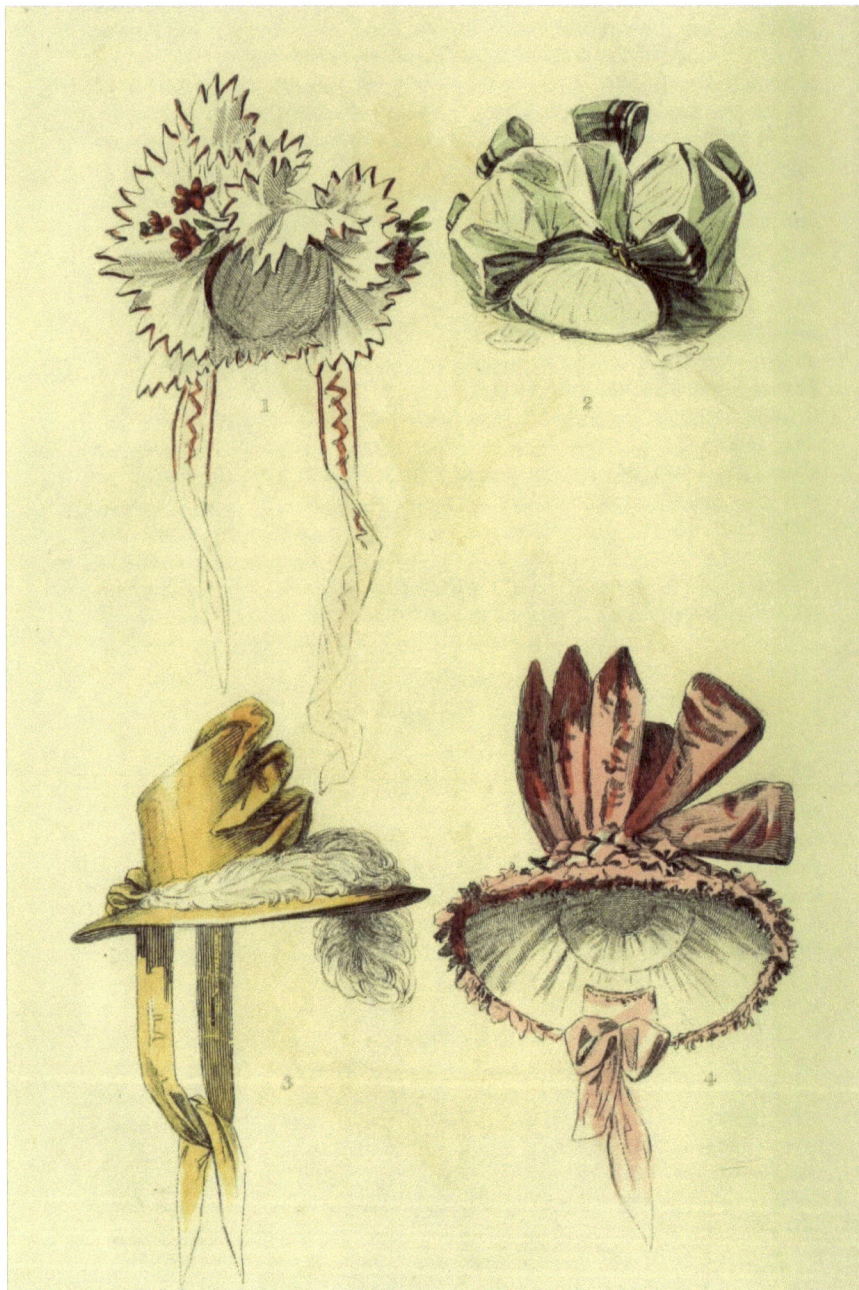

Head-Dresses
October 1828

HEAD-DRESSES

1. Cap of white *crèpe lisse*, the border very broad, vandyked and edged with scarlet braiding; in a deep puff on the left temple a cardinal flower is placed; the border touches the forehead in front, takes a retrograde direction and rises high on the right side, and is sustained with another branch of the cardinal flower: the head-piece is bound with scarlet satin.

2. Toque of Parisian gauze of a pale Pomona green, folded very deep and standing up from the head-piece, and adorned with several long bows of broad green gauze ribbon; the crown is low and circular.

3. Hat of Aurora or amber-colour *gros de Naples*; the crown higher in front than behind, and the front of the brim very projecting and shallow at the back, where a small bow is placed, to which a long white ostrich feather is fastened; it lies flat on the brim, and falls below it towards the left or opposite side; a zig-zag puff trimming ornaments the front; broad amber-colour strings.

4. *Capóte* of rose-colour silk, trimmed with a notched *ruche* at the edge of the brim, and lined with white sarsnet; the crown is high, and in front has two very large stiffened bows like long loops and a triplet of leaves standing erect.

Evening Dress
October 1828

EVENING DRESS

Dress of sea-green *crèpe de Lyons*; the bodice made close to the shape with perpendicular plaits formed by a corded seam into a stomacher, ornamented with buttons of the same colour down the front and back; the tucker a narrow *ruche* of tulle. The sleeves are *à la Marie*, being short and full, with one division formed by a sea-green satin band round the arm, and fastened by a garnet snap, and another band and snap at the termination of the sleeve. The skirt is fulled in all round the waist, and has two flounces a quarter of a yard each in depth, edged with crimson satin; ornaments of a fan-like shape extend half way over each flounce. The hair is divided in front *à la Madonna*, and has plaited bands of hair on the left side, and several rows of pearls on the right, terminating with a fancy ornament, behind which a cluster of ringlets descends; three large bows of hair and, rose-colour gauze adorn the summit of the head. Necklace composed of a double row, the upper of garnets set in gold, with a handsome medallion snap in front; the second row is a wreath of embossed gold leaves, with pendant pearls; earrings to correspond; broad enamelled bracelets outside the white kid gloves, which are stamped and drawn at the elbow; white satin shoes and sandals.

Promenade Dress
November 1828

PROMENADE DRESS

Dress of black satin *Turque*; the bodice made close and long-waisted, laced before and behind, and also pointed: the sleeves are very large to the elbow, and twice confined with black velvet bands, fastened by jet buckles. The sleeves are smaller from the elbow to the wrist, and are there confined by Berlin cameo bracelets of cast iron. The skirt is very full, and plaited in all round, and trimmed with a puffing of black *crèpe lisse* and lanceola-leaves, pointing upwards: *chemisette* within the dress, and full *ruche*. Large circular hat of black Leghorn, tied under the chin on the right side with trimming, irradiating from thence to the edge of the brim; papilionaceous bows of black gauze ribbon are placed on each side towards the top of the crown. Lavender-colour gloves; black prunella shoes; Thibet shawl, of lavender-colour.

Dinner Dress
November 1828

DINNER DRESS

Black velvet dress, made extremely simple; the body *à la Rosalinde*, scolloped round the bust, with pendant ornaments attached to the point of each scallop: melon velvet sleeves under long full ones of white aërophane crape, fastened at the wrist by jet bracelets, nearly half-a-quarter broad. The skirt is fulled in round the waist, and terminated by scollops instead of a hem or rouleau. Turban of white aërophane crape; the fulness longitudinal, and supported by frequent bands of black and lavender-colour velvet; band of the same round the head, and a plume of white ostrich feathers and fancy velvet ornament placed far back on the left side. The hair in ringlets. White kid gloves, stamped and tied at the wrist. Black satin shoes.

Promenade Dress
December 1828

PROMENADE DRESS

Pelisse of lavender-colour satin *Turque*; the body made high and close to the shape, with a circular stiffened collar, rather open, and displaying a very full *ruche* of British tulle. The sleeves are very full as far as the gauntlet cuff, which is of black velvet, ornamented with a branch of laurel, arranged perpendicularly. The pelisse fastens in front, and is trimmed from the throat with rich black velvet, deeply notched or vandyked on the outside, and a border of the same nearly half a yard broad. Black velvet hat, of a closer shape than those worn in the summer, lined with lavender-colour satin, and corded at the edge of the brim with the same; large bows of black velvet and lavender-colour satin ribbon decorate the crown, which is rather low and circular: the strings are long, sometimes loose, but more frequently tied to confine the hat. Cap of tulle; the border very full, and continued under the chin in the cottage style. The hair is parted in front, and arranged in large curls. Lavender-colour gloves; black shoes of *gros des Indes*.

Evening Costume
December 1828

EVENING COSTUME

Orange-colour dress of Parisian gauze, with satin stripes of the same colour, and lozenge ornaments of red and green. The body is made low and *en draperie*, the fulness confined by a small corded band in the centre of the front and back; an orange-colour satin cape, sinuated towards the top, rises from the *ceinture*, and is terminated on the shoulder by a satin bow. The sleeves are short and full, with inside stiffenings to keep them in form. The skirt is without gores, and gathered in very full all round the waist, and is ornamented with pyramidal trimmings as high as the knee, cut bias, and made very full, edged with a piping of satin, and one of similar breadth down the centre, with a bouquet of roses at the summit of each pyramid: beneath is a satin rouleau. Orange-colour satin sash and a slip of the same colour is worn with the dress. The hair is parted in front and in ringlets, dressed very high, with plaited bands, and an ornamented comb at the top. White kid gloves, stamped at the elbow; hair-bracelets, with snaps of burnished and dead gold; gold tissue shoes.

GLOSSARY

Names and their meanings, like fashions, change with the times. The definitions in this glossary are meant to explain the terms in the context of the period covered in this book, 1818–28. Some may seem farfetched or excessive, others so obscure as to defy definition today, but this was not unusual for an age so wrapped in romanticism that ordinary language seemed less than adequate and too prosaic for the needs of fashion.

Aërophane crape. A fine, airy, crimped crepe, almost transparent

À Feodore. An obscure term used with reference to satin. Possibly derived from Feodore, an officer of the ancient Court of Wards.

Aigrette. Tuft or plume of feathers.

Ailes de papillon. Cloth ornaments arranged to suggest the wings of a butterfly.

À la biret. In the style of a beret or a biretta.

À la blouse. Wide, ample, full, unconfined.

À la Farinet. Reference of term obscure, probably meaning raised like die-cut surface.

À la Flamande. In the Flemish manner, in this series applying to long, dangling earrings.

À la Madonna. A hairstyle, center-parted and simply arranged, like that of Madonnas in Italian paintings.

À la Marie Stuart. Hats or bonnets dipping to a point in front, a style associated with the headdresses worn by Marie Stuart, Queen of Scots (1542–87).

À la militaire. In the military style.

À la Van Dyke. In the styles recorded in the paintings by Van Dyck (1599–1641).

À l'antique. In the manner of the Greeks of antiquity.

À l'Espagnol. In the Spanish style, referring to the slashes of the 16th century and the fitted bolices of women's costumes of the 16th and 17th centuries.

Athenian braces. Bands of soft folds emulating Greek drapery.

À trois pièces. In three parts.

Bandeau (pl. bandeaux). A narrow band worn either on the head or on the costume for decorative purposes.

Barège. Very fine material, generally of silk and wool, with silk thrown to the surface giving the fabric a silky, foamy texture.

Black du cape. Term obscure, possibly a special fabric used for millinery.

Blond lace. A lace made of fine mesh with patterns worked in silk producing shiny satin-like pattern. Blond lace could be natural colored, black or, occasionally, in other colors such as green.

Bombasine. A textile having a twilled appearance with a silk warp and a worsted weft. It was usually black and, because it was lusterless, was often used for mourning.

Book muslin. A cotton fabric with a shiny surface similar to sateen. It was so called because it was often used to face the inside covers of books.

Bouffant. A puff.

Bouillonnée. Puffed or bubbling out.

Brides. Ribbon on bonnets resembling bridle reins.

Brussels sprigs. Floral sprays of Brussels lace, often mounted on machine-made net.

Buckinghamshire. Bobbin lace worked in one piece on a pillow.

Cambric. Very fine thin linen.

Capote. A bonnet with a firm brim and a soft head-shaped crown.

Capuchin. A hood worn by monks; also for out-of-doors use in the 16th, 17th and 18th centuries.

Cashemire (cashmere). A soft woolen fabric with a twill weave originally imported from Kashmir and made of the under hair of Tibetan goats. Later it was imitated in Europe.

Ceinture. Sash, belt, waistband.

Chamois. Soft, pliable leather from chamois (goatlike antelopes) as well as from sheep and goats.

Chemisette. A dickey or fill-in for a low-cut bodice, usually made of fine linen or cotton and often lace trimmed.

Chip. A very coarse straw used especially in women's hats and bonnets.

Circassian cloth. Thin worsted fabric named after Circassia, an area in the Caucasus.

Collerette. Small, usually fancy collar.

Coquelicot. The color poppy red.

Coquings. Shell-shaped trimmings.

Corded point. Point lace (lace made with a needle) and decorated with cording.

Cornette. A bonnet-style day cap, usually made of fine cotton or linen. Worn alone at home or under hats out-of-doors.

Corsage. Bodice or upper part of a women's dress.

Corsage à la soubrette. Bodice in the style of a lady's maid's costume. In the early 19th century, it probably included a corselet like that worn by country girls.

Corsage en [or à la] blouse. Bodice with loose folds or pleats.

Coul (Caul). A cap shaped like the caul or membrane that sometimes covers an infant's head at birth.

Couleur d'oreille d'ours. Color of polyanthus, the oxlip or some variety of narcissus.

Couleur monstre. A green color attributed to monsters or fantastic mythological creatures.

Crape (French crêpe). A thin, crinkled silk, cotton or wool.

Crêpe lisse. A silk gauze without crimping.

Demi-cornette. A sheer day cap that does not fully cover the head and is often worn with a hat or bonnet.

Demi-toilette. A cap or garment worn primarily at home but is not quite a negligee.

Easing. Edge trimming done with puckering, shirring or clipping.

Emarginate. With notched margins.

En bouffants. In puffs or puffed out.

En bouffes. In puffs.

En bride. Ribbons arranged like bridle reins.

En carreaux. In small squares, lozenges or diamond shapes.

En gigot. Sleeves shaped like a leg of mutton with fullness at the shoulder narrowing toward the wrist.

En grandes bouches. Large curls.

En serpent. Serpentine.

En treillis. Like latticework.

En tuyau. With a stem attached.

Étrangère. Unusual, strange, foreign.

Farinet. See À la farinet.

Fichu. Kerchief or small scarf, generally of thin, filmy material, that was worn around the neckline.

Folia peltata. Leaves with stems attached to the underneath part instead of to the edges.

French work. Whitework, including white-on-white embroidery, combined with cut and pierced designs.

Gigot de mouton. Literally, leg of mutton, referring to sleeve shapes which are large at the shoulder and fit closely at the wrist.

Gofre crape. Crinkled, fluted or pleated crepe.

Grenadine. A silk or silk-and-wool mixture woven with an open mesh. Grenadine can be plain or figured.

Gros de Berlin. Ribbed fabric, probably of wool.

Gros de Naples. An Italian silk with corded surface.

Gros des Indes. A heavy silk having a stripe formed transversely to its length.

Honiton. Lace in the Brussels style made in Honiton.

Jaconet (Jàcconet). A thin cotton fabric somewhat like muslin.

Jane. Possibly "jean," a sateen with a twill weave.

Jocko. Monkey or ape of great intelligence, hero of numerous 19th-century stage productions, portrayed by a man.

Kerseymere. A fine woolen fabric with a twill weave having a special texture with one third of work threads above and the rest below.

Lappets. Bands or streamers of lace arranged on the sides of the head with ends left pendent.

Leghorn. A plaited Italian wheat straw used in hats.

Letting-in lace. Bands of lace with spaces left open through which ribbons could be threaded.

Levantine. A twilled soft silk with a shiny surface.

Likanian. Term obscure, possibly referring to Lydian- or Phrygian-style cap.

Limeric (Limerick). A glove leather of very fine quality.

Love ribbon. A ribbon of gauze striped with satin.

Lutestring. A glossy silk woven with very fine cording.

Mancherons. Sleeve trimming at the wrists or at the shoulders like epaulettes.

Marabouts (marabou). Soft tail or wing feathers from the marabou stork.

Mull. A very fine, delicate muslin.

Nankeen. A yellowish-brown cotton material.

Navarino. Seaport in southeastern Greece, also called Pylos.

Noeud. A bow or knot.

Parisian mob. A full round cap of fine linen or cotton with a puffed crown and a ruffled border.

Pelerine. A cape-collar or short cape, matching or contrasting.

Pelisse. An outdoor garment such as a coat or cloak.

Plaited. Pleats in cloth; braids in hair.

Pluche (plush). A fabric of silk or wool with a high pile.

Ponceau. Poppy red.

Quadrille feathers. An obscure term, possibly referring to one of four groups of horsemen in a carousel or tournament, each wearing a special colorful costume.

Quilling. Small round pleats sewn lightly to remain open in flute-like folds.

Reticule. Lady's small handbag.

Rouleau (pl. rouleaux). A strip of fabric loosely stuffed into a tube-like shape and used to trim dresses, generally at the hem.

Round gown or dress. A closed one-piece dress.

Ruche. Pleated or closely ruffled strip of lace, net or some soft fabric to be used as trimming.

Sarsnet (sarcenet). A thin silk with a taffeta weave and a slight sheen.

Soie de Londres. Satin or satin-like silk.

Sontag sleeves. Sleeves with fullness confined at intervals by bands. Also called *à la Marie.*

Spanish puffs. Origin of term unclear. Possibly a reference to decorations on Spanish 17th-century costumes.

Spencer. A short jacket, often of contrasting color or material, and ending at a high waistline just below the bust.

Stomacher. A V-shaped inset in the front of the bodice.

Tartarian. In the style of a Tartar's turban.

Thibet cloth. Imitation cashmere made in Paisley, Scotland.

Tippet. A scarf.

Toque. A close-fitting brimless hat.

Toque de Ninon. A toque, possibly in the style of Ninon de Lenclos, a fashionable French lady (1620–1705).

Torsade. A twisted fringe, cord or ribbon used for trimming.

Tucker. A lace or lawn edging used (tucked in) around a low-cut neckline.

Turque. Brilliant soft woolen fabric.

Urling's lace or net. Machine-made lace or net of Urling's Patent Thread, developed in 1817.

Urling's velours natté. Velvet with a twisted nap.

Vandyke (adj. vandyked). A pointed tooth-like border of lace or other material similar to those in the works of Van Dyck (1599–1641).

Velours épingle. Terry velvet.

Velours natté. See Urling's velours natté.

Velours simulé. Simulated velvet.

Wadded. Padded with cotton batting.

Zephyr. A light, very fine, silky cotton.

Zephyrne. Light-weight fabric of silk or wool.

JODY GAYLE, bestselling author and researcher, likens her work to that of a literary archeologist rather than a traditional author or imperator of history. She is dedicated to unearthing publications of the past, and sharing these long-forgotten books... the jewels and riches of the written word. She has uncovered tens of thousands of old publications from the eighteenth and nineteenth centuries and wants to bring them to life, and send her readers traveling back in time.

About Jody...

* She grew up on a farm in a small town of about 500 people and first learned to drive on a tractor. She can milk a cow as easily as pluck a chicken.

* Stood within twenty feet of the first node of the International Space Station. Unfortunately, her feet were firmly planted on the earth at the time.

* Has gone whitewater rafting and horseback riding in the mountains of Montana. She has swum with dolphins and sharks, and refueled a fighter jet in the sky on an Air Force KC135. Jody is a bit of an adventurer.

* Jody and her son share the same birthday -- New Year's Day!

She loves to hear from her readers. Visit her website and Facebook page.

Thank you for reading
FASHIONS IN THE ERA OF JANE AUSTEN

If you enjoyed this book, I would appreciate it if you'd help other readers enjoy it, too. After all, most books are purchased due to word-of-mouth recommendations. How can you help?

Recommend it. Please help other readers find this book by recommending it to friends, readers' groups, and discussion boards.

Review it. Please tell other readers why you liked this book by reviewing it on Amazon, Goodreads, or your blog. If you write a review, please send me a copy at jody@jodygayle.com